Social and Economic Factors in Spending for Public Education

JERRY MINER is Associate Professor of Economics at Syracuse University, now on leave at UNESCO, where he is engaged in research on the economics of education. Professor Miner was an undergraduate and graduate student at the University of Michigan, where he was on the staff of the Survey Research Center.

The Economics and Politics of Public Education 11

17184

Social and Economic Factors in Spending for Public Education

JERRY MINER

SYRACUSE UNIVERSITY PRESS SU 1963

This study was made possible in part by funds granted by Carnegie Corporation of New York. The statements made and views expressed are solely the responsibility of the author.

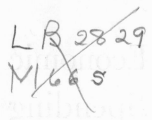

Manufactured in the United States of America by
The Heffernan Press Inc., Worcester, Mass.

Library of Congress Catalog Card: 63-11011

Contents

Tables

Preface

IN THE United States today, more than ever before, decisions by governments determine the use of economic resources for nonmilitary purposes. Increased recognition and understanding of the role of government in the economic life of the nation and the greatly heightened interdependence characteristic of a modern industrial society have combined to produce a dual economic system in which the allocation of resources that results from consumer and business decisions is accompanied, to a considerable extent, by public administration of resources. Study of the goals of public bodies and of the factors that influence their behavior makes possible forecasts of government actions and evaluations of this performance—two elements necessary for the formulation of public policy.

This monograph investigates local school governments, which have major responsibility for the administration of the largest nonmilitary functional area of public spending. Criteria for appropriate levels of expenditure for public elementary and secondary education are examined here, together with a search for the empirical regularities that underlie expenditure patterns of different school governments. For economists the primary interest of this study is in the application of contemporary economic views of the normative theory of public expenditures to spending for public education, and in the application of methods developed for the empirical analysis of consumer and business behavior to the behavior of the body politic. For educators and students of educational finance primary interest may lie more in the approach here to educational expenditures as a process of allocating scarce resources by means of the political process, and in the specific findings regarding the sources of variation in spending among local schools.

I have received the help of many persons and organizations in the preparation of this study. I am grateful to Dr. Virgil R. Walker, Director of the Educational Statistics Branch of the U.S. Office of Education, and his colleagues for the data they provided, and to Robert Fairbanks, who supervised the computer runs. To my assistant, Douglas Wilson, goes deep appreciation for many painstaking jobs which included the adjustment of census data for non-coterminous school systems and a detailed reading of the manuscript that led to a great number of improvements in substance and style. Walter Mc-Mahon's suggestions clarified the organization of the monograph and helped to sharpen the relationship to economic theory of large portions of the study. Comments by Thomas James served to resolve several issues dealing with state aid programs and other educational matters. Edna Hockensmith typed numerous drafts of the manuscript. Jesse Burkhead provided encouragement, patience, and assistance, at times over a considerable distance. Eugene McLoone and Seymour Sacks contributed comments and suggestions on data and analytical techniques. The Syracuse University Computing Center, and in particular Otway O. Pardee, Director, and William Overholt were most generous in extending time and facilities.

The shortcomings which remain are entirely my responsibility. I hope, however, that the displeasure occasioned by these shortcomings will be manifest by efforts to remedy them through the further development of an operational theory that can be used to reveal the effects on levels of public expenditure of changes in demographic and economic characteristics and of different governmental arrangements.

Paris, France   Jerry Miner
Spring, 1963

I. The Objectives of the Study

THIS MONOGRAPH examines the determinants of expenditures for elementary and secondary public education. With a focus on the local government which administers public schools, it seeks both to develop the economic reasoning involved in determining optimum levels of spending for public education and to identify the factors that influence actual spending by local school systems. The first of these objectives is implemented by the application of principles of social economy to the development of criteria for public expenditures in general and educational spending in particular. The examination of the determinants of actual public spending for education contains, first, a review of the major empirical studies that attempt to specify the legal, economic, social, political, and other factors that influence levels of spending by individual government units. Secondly, a major aspect of the monograph is an empirical study of the factors that influence school spending in a sample of 1,100 local school systems in 23 states.

THE MAGNITUDE AND VARIABILITY OF LOCAL SCHOOL EXPENDITURES

During the 1959-1960 school year about $15 billion was spent for local schools by all levels of government in the United States. Of this total, three-quarters was for current operating expenses and the remainder for capital outlays and debt service—mostly for construction and new equipment. Since the major responsibilities for providing public schools are delegated by the states to officials of more than 42,000 separate local school systems, over $14.5 billion of the $15 billion spent for local schools was administered under the aegis of local governments. State grants to local school systems amounted to about 40 per cent of these expenditures and the federal government provided about $650 million more. Expenditures for local public schools in the United States thus constituted roughly 10 per cent of the total of about $150 billion spent by all levels of government in 1960. Except for national defense, local education is the largest single functional category of public spending.

In the United States neither is there central control over educational spending, nor are educational standards set by the federal government. As a result there is great variation in expenditure not only from one state to another but also among the school systems within each state. Some of this variation is attributable to cost differentials which require different outlays to provide similar educational services. For the most part, however, expenditure variations reflect genuine differences in the caliber of educational services provided. The average national per capita current operating expenditures for local public schools in 1959-1960 was about $63. Variations among states are considerable; at one extreme, Mississippi, Arkansas, Alabama, and Kentucky spent less than $45 per capita, while expenditures in Wyoming, Alaska, and California were over $83 per capita. Differences in current operating expenditures per pupil enrolled are even more pronounced. The average in 1959-1960 was $345 per pupil; Mississippi spent $177 per pupil and Arkansas and Alabama spent less than $220 per pupil, whereas New York spent $484 per pupil, and per pupil spending in California, Oregon, New Jersey, and Wyoming exceeded $400.[1]

Statewide figures, however, are only averages of expenditures of individual local school systems. It is, after all, the amount of these local expenditures which determines the educational services provided to pupils. Table 1 presents selected data regarding variations in spending within certain states. These data indicate that variations in local school expenditures within states differ greatly from state to state. In some states such as Arkansas, Louisiana, New York, and Ohio the range of variations within the state exceeds the range of average expenditure among states. But in other states such as Alabama and Massachusetts the range between the highest and lowest spending districts is quite narrow and falls well within the limits of the observed variation among states.

A major purpose of this study is to explain the reasons for differences in local school expenditures. The examination of sources of variation in expenditures encompasses both school systems located within a state and those located in different states.

---

[1] Itemized per capita current operation expenditures for local schools by states are presented in Table 18 of *Governmental Finances in 1960*, U.S. Bureau of the Census (Washington, 1961). Expenditures per pupil enrolled have been calculated from data in this same table along with information from Table 4 of *Public School Systems in 1960*, U.S. Bureau of the Census (Washington, 1960).

TABLE 1

PER CAPITA AND PER PUPIL EXPENDITURES FOR LOCAL SCHOOLS,
SELECTED STATES

State	Per Capita Expenditures of State and Local Gov'ts	Range of Countywide Per Capita Expenditures	Per Pupil Expenditures of State and Local Gov'ts	Range of School System Per Pupil Expenditures
California	$112	$57–$162	$492	$289–$683
New York	96	63– 164	585	437– 704
Connecticut	81	49– 96	420	247– 596
Louisiana	81	37– 129	370	273– 560
Pennsylvania	80	38– 110	421	309– 502
Ohio	74	27– 141	388	206– 612
Massachusetts	64	49– 97	413	103– 948
Georgia	61	5– 76	236	163– 341
Rhode Island	58	47– 66	417	271– 705
South Carolina	54	30– 74	223	135– 204

SOURCE: U.S. Bureau of the Census, *Local Government Finances and Employment in Relation to Population, 1957* (Washington, 1961); National Education Association, *Rankings of the States, 1961* (Washington, 1961); available annual reports from state departments of education for recent years from 1957 to 1960.

THE SOCIAL AND ECONOMIC IMPORTANCE OF EDUCATION

The over-all economic effect of the large amount of public spending for education is an indication of its importance for study. An annual stream of spending of over $15 billion has a great impact on the national economy both in generating aggregate income and employment and in influencing directly the purposes for which scarce resources are used. Virtually all spending for education is resource-using public expenditure. Providing educational services uses up scarce labor, capital, and land and precludes their use for other purposes. Public outlays for highways, hospitals, and many other governmental services are also resource-using, but government spending for welfare payments, interest on government debt, and social insurance benefits merely places income in the hands of individuals who then purchase whatever goods and services they choose. These transfer payments reflect government decisions about the distribution of income, but do not involve public decisions about alternative resource use. A striking illustration of the quantity of resources used in public education is the 1.8 million people employed (measured in full-time equivalents) in local public schools in 1960 which amounted to close to 30 per cent of total government civilian employment in the United

States in that year and to about 3 per cent of total civilian employment.

The provision of education influences pupils and nonpupils and future as well as present generations. Education yields direct benefits to students not only by increasing their lifetime earning capacities but also by enabling them to be more aware of the full range of human experience. Furthermore, spending for education yields more than a current dividend; it is an investment in human capital which, like physical capital, results in increased output per unit of input. Thus, spending for schools increases national productivity. To make the most of resources it is necessary that outlays for education not be halted short of the point where the gains in productivity, resulting from further educational spending, are greater than the costs of additional funds, measured in terms of the value of alternative uses of these resources.

Proponents of increased educational outlays insist that a well-educated public has great political and social value which accrues not only to those going to a particular school, or to their families, or to those in the community or state where a school is located, but to almost all members of society. Moreover, education is indispensable in providing the equality of opportunity which is the major characteristic of an equalitarian society. High levels of educational services must be available free of direct charge and on a compulsory basis to all who can benefit if power and privilege are not to determine educational attainment and thus make a mockery of equality of opportunity. The extent to which resources are committed to education is therefore crucial to a nation's welfare.

The second major purpose of this study is critical evaluation of the economic issues involved in determining optimum levels of expenditures for elementary and secondary education and the best arrangements for financing them.

IMPLICATIONS OF THE STUDY

A satisfactory answer to an inquiry into the determinants of educational expenditures has considerable value for policy purposes. If the effects of demographic, economic, social, psychological, and other factors over which policy makers have virtually no control can be taken into account, policy decisions can be based on clear-cut expectations. Furthermore, such knowledge will make it possible to estimate the net effect of "policy parameters" such as dependent versus independent school district organization or alternative formulas for state aid to education. At the same time, reliable estimates of the effects of non–policy-determined elements (e.g., population growth) reveal the consequences of anticipated developments and make possible more reliable advanced planning.

Because current projections show future educational needs substantially outstripping anticipated tax revenues from existing resources during the next decade, information about the financial consequences of educational policies is especially important. There is little doubt that resources are adequate to meet anticipated educational needs;[2] the problem is to develop policies and techniques that will channel these resources into public education. If additional resources are needed, knowledge of those educational policies which lead to higher levels of school spending is crucial. Furthermore, estimates of the impact on educational expenditures of anticipated or projected changes in factors such as enrollments, costs, and property valuation provide a basis for more effective use of whatever amount of the resources are available to administrators of local schools.

Knowledge of the trend of current educational developments and of the consequences of specific educational policies must be integrated with concepts of social economy and other social goals if proper policy choices are to be made. Ultimate standards for evaluating particular educational policies are value judgments. But, given certain objectives, the social scientist often can evaluate the degree to which different policies conform to the standard. The application of the principles of social economy to the relationship between policies and goals in the use of resources for education must also be an integral part of decision-making in local school governments.

Chapter II discusses the relationships of public spending for elementary and secondary education to the general theory of ideal levels of public expenditures. The major concern here is to describe the relationship of outlays for education to the achievement of social economy in the use of resources. The third chapter is a detailed review and critique of the principal empirical studies of the determinants of public spending. Brief discussions of the methodology of the empirical analysis of public spending and of studies dealing with expenditures for all functions is followed by a more complete analysis of investigations of public spending for education.

The fourth and fifth chapters present the details of statistical analysis of current expenditures by local school governments. Chapter

---

[2] Jesse Burkhead, *State and Local Taxes for Public Education,* in this series, discusses the question of needs and resources for public education.

IV sets forth the rationale for this study and a description of the variables used. Results and conclusions are discussed in Chapter V.

Finally, Chapter VI is a brief summary of the major issues and the extent to which they appear to be resolved by this study.

II. Education and the Theory of Public Expenditures

T HE MIXED ECONOMY of the United States is primarily oriented toward private production and individual consumption. Still, in 1961, governmental units in the United States spent over $150 billion and collected only slightly less in revenues. What is the rationale for public outlays that amount to almost 30 per cent of the national product? Are there guidelines for determining "optimum" purposes and levels of governmental outlays? How does public spending for elementary and secondary education fit into the general explanation of public expenditures? This chapter discusses these questions, beginning with a description of the essential features of a market economy and the principles of social economy that indicate the most appropriate use of resources. These principles are then used to demarcate the role of government in a consumer-directed economic system. The chapter concludes with an analysis of the provision of educational services in the light of this framework. At many points, however, issues are raised which cannot be resolved by recourse to generally accepted concepts governing the efficient use of resources. The resolution of such issues, which involve value judgments, is a matter of personal evaluation and does not rest on the same foundation as does the logic of the principles of social economy.

PUBLIC EXPENDITURES AND THE MARKET ECONOMY

The Operation of a Market Economy

The economic system of the United States is essentially a market economy in which hundreds of thousands of private firms produce goods and services which are sold to millions of individual consumers at specified prices. Ideally, this highly decentralized system, based on the use of prices, allocates scarce resources to uses that most satisfy the desires of consumers.

In a market economy business firms seeking profits purchase and transform privately owned land, labor, and capital goods into final products. The uses of these factors of production in a consumer-

7

directed economy are determined by individual preferences revealed by the prices consumers are willing to pay for various amounts of different commodities. The prices at which different commodities can be sold act as guides to producers and indicate what products are most desired by society. Producers, motivated by a desire for profits, combine the factors of production into those commodities which can be sold at the highest prices. Producers will bid for the services performed by a factor in accordance with its productivity in different uses and the prices at which the commodities produced from it can be sold. The result of this decentralized process is a system of control and coordination in which factors of production are used to provide those commodities most desired by the individual members of society. At the same time a competitive market promotes flexible prices so that quantities provided tend to equal quantities demanded, and there are no lasting shortages or accumulations of particular commodities. Furthermore, the distribution of final products is also determined, because the prices paid to factor owners combined with the quantities of factors supplied determine individual incomes which, in turn, decide the share of output going to particular persons or families.

In an "ideal" or "perfect" market economy two kinds of "efficiencies" prevail when scarce resources are used in accordance with consumer preferences. Only if all products are produced by techniques that use the least possible amounts of scarce resources does an economic system get the most out of its resources. This requirement of least-cost output is called productive or technological efficiency, and is achieved in a market economy when entrepreneurs, in trying to maximize profits, choose productive techniques to minimize costs. But least-cost production does not ensure an optimum use of resources. The right final products, that is, those that consumers want, must be produced at least cost. The dovetailing of production and consumer preferences is called economic efficiency, and is attained in an ideal market when entrepreneurs provide those products in those quantities which yield the greatest margin between total receipts and total costs when costs are minimized. Since total revenue for a given quantity of any product depends upon its price, which is a reflection of consumers' evaluation of the want-satisfying capacity of the goods in question, producers in seeking to maximize profits are providing precisely the goods consumers most want and are achieving both economic and technological efficiency.

Technological and economic efficiency are not independent of each other. Technological efficiency depends upon economic efficiency because technological efficiency means producing at least cost and does not mean using the fewest number of physical units of factors. Producing at lowest cost requires taking into account relative factor costs and technological possibilities. Since the cost of a particular factor depends upon consumers' evaluations of the different products that could be produced with the factor, ultimately consumer preferences determine relative factor costs and hence the resources used in producing particular products.

Economic efficiency is influenced by technological efficiency because consumer demand depends on the distribution of income among individuals with different preferences. The technological requirements of production are among the determinants of producers' demand for factors and thereby influence the incomes going to particular factor owners. The determination, then, of equilibrium values for prices and quantities of commodities and factors in a perfect market economy is a highly interrelated process in which the final result takes into account the scarcities of factors of production relative to their want-satisfying capacities mediated by existing knowledge of the transformation of inputs into outputs.

Competition among producers is crucial for the effective operation of a market economy. The entry of new entrepreneurs and shifting of established producers in less profitable fields into profitable industries insures that resources will be used for those products consumers most demand. This process causes prices to tend toward a level equal to production costs plus an adequate return to invested funds. Competition among factor owners also is important for efficient use of resources. Factor prices that are maintained above competitive levels restrict the use of such factors by producers, who instead use lower-priced substitutes which are really more scarce than the noncompetitive factor. As a result, the social costs of production are increased.

The major implication of this discussion is that the real cost of any final commodity actually produced is the foregone product or products which could have been produced by using the same resources in other productive processes. Fundamentally, the choice among alternative uses of scarce resources hinges on how society values the various commodities which can be made out of certain combinations of resources and how these values are communicated to those making decisions about production. Technology determines the range of possibilities and the quantities of resources required, but in a market economy choices among the possibilities depend on consumers' preferences. The market is an institutional arrangement by which individual preferences are manifested through demand-prices and determine, within the range of technical possibilities, which commodities and what quantities of them shall be produced.[1]

Problems Requiring Government Action

This short characterization of a consumer-guided market economy suggests not only the virtues of a decentralized economy but some of its inadequacies as well.

Maintaining Competition. If competition among producers and factor owners is not maintained, resources will not be utilized to provide the most satisfaction possible. Substantial departures from competition usually mean that producers in one industry are able to earn profits in excess of those available in other industries. Under these circumstances shifting resources into the production of more profitable commodities would add more to consumer satisfaction than the resulting decrease in output in less profitable enterprises would deduct from satisfaction. The existence of monopoly power hampers the entry of additional producers and prevents a more socially desirable use of resources. Also, the excessive profits characteristic of monopolistic industries distort the distribution of income and concentrate command over final goods in the hands of those who have not created commensurate amounts of socially useful product.

One important function of government in a market economy is to maintain competition where possible and provide a competitive-like solution to the use of resources when competition is impossible for technological or other reasons. Certain commodities such as telephone service or electric power involve production and distribution processes such that a single producer can supply the needs of an entire community. Competition in the provision of such services is wasteful and unstable. Here government endeavors to provide a competitive-like price and rate of return for such commodities by regulating the operation of these industries while leaving their ownership in private hands. Where competitive markets are feasible, government attempts to keep monopolistic forces in check by enacting and enforcing antitrust legislation.

It is important to note that maintaining a degree of competition in the economy involves only small public expenditures. Preventing

[1] For a more comprehensive nontechnical discussion of the operation of an ideal market economy see Howard R. Bowen, *Toward Social Economy* (New York: Rinehart and Company, Inc., 1948), especially Chapters 13-16.

and regulating monopoly is often referred to in terms of the government's role as an umpire to assure that the players adhere to the rules of the economic game.

Satisfaction of Social Wants. Even if the competitive rules of the game are enforced, a market economy will not produce adequate amounts of certain kinds of goods and services demanded by consumers. This deficiency arises primarily because part or all of the benefits of some commodities are received regardless of whether a particular consumer pays for them or not. For example, a national defense program will confer whatever benefits it provides to virtually all residents of a nation, and there is no way of allocating the costs of missiles and troops in accordance with the benefits they yield to particular individuals. Commodities of this sort are called "social goods." Social goods have two distinctive features. One is that they are jointly consumed in that one person's use does not preclude another's use of the same commodity. The other is the impossibility of excluding nonpayers from obtaining substantial benefits. Such goods will not be provided by private business firms producing for profit because consumers have no reason to pay for them since nonpayment does not exclude them from enjoying the benefits. Nonetheless, these kinds of commodities are desired by individual consumers in much the same way as private goods are demanded. People want scarce resources to be used for national defense and other social goods as well as for food, clothing, and automobiles.[2]

There are many goods and services which, to a considerable degree, share these two distinctive features of social goods. National defense, the services of a lighthouse, and the functions of a national judiciary are illustrations of such services. Other traditional public functions such as public parks, public education, fire and police protection, involve, to a lesser but still significant degree, elements of "joint consumption" and an inability to exclude nonpayers from gaining benefits.

Although benefits gained from these quasi-collective services are obtained by others than those directly using the facilities, private provision of them is possible. Admission fees could be charged for recreation areas; fire protection and police protection could be bought by individuals, families, and businesses; all education could be conducted in private schools charging tuition. Such arrangements, how-

[2] The most thorough discussion of the concept of social goods is in Richard A. Musgrave, *The Theory of Public Finance* (New York: McGraw-Hill, 1959), Chapters 1 and 4.

ever, would provide only as much of these services as would satisfy the demands of those directly using them and would not take into account the benefits received by persons other than the immediate consumer. In education, for example, the desire of the family for a child's education is reflected in its private demand for education, but the desires of other members of the community for the benefits of a well-educated citizenry play no part in the demand for education by the child's family. Educational demand will be understated if private provision of education is dominant. Similar considerations pertain to police and fire protection: neighbors benefit when fires are prevented from spreading and criminals, once apprehended, cannot victimize other families. Yet the private demand of each family reflects only its personal evaluation of the protective service.

One solution to the nonproduction of "pure" social goods and the inadequate provision of goods yielding substantial social benefits is to provide them through the budget principle rather than the market principle. The market principle fails to provide pure or nearly pure social goods because consumers will not voluntarily pay for services whose benefits they can obtain, in approximately equal amounts, without paying. The market principle based on a *quid pro quo* relationship between consumer and producer requires that consumers voluntarily pay producers in exchange for the goods they receive. Through this exchange consumers obtain the goods which yield the satisfactions they crave, and producers recoup their production costs and compensation for their entrepreneurial efforts. But, if the product is such that producers cannot restrict satisfactions to those who buy their goods, pecuniary exchange becomes impossible, producers cannot recoup even their costs, and incentive for private production is nonexistent. Even when sale by private producers to those consumers who gain substantially more satisfaction than others is feasible, the market principle fails to register the benefits to non-buyers and consequently provides insufficient quantities of these kinds of commodities.

The budget principle is an alternative to the voluntary exchange of money for commodities between consumer and producer. Here, goods and services are provided to consumers free of direct charge by government and payment for these commodities is made out of compulsory levies upon the consumers. Under the budget principle all consumers have equal access to the publicly provided goods, and ideally the taxes levied upon different consumers vary in relation to the satisfaction they derive from the commonly used services.

According to the budget principle the quantities of particular services provided are based on consumers' demands for alternative uses of the economy's limited resources. In this context each household in a community is viewed as having a schedule of the amounts it is willing to pay to obtain a given number of units of a particular publicly provided good or service. These schedules or demand curves depend upon household incomes, preferences, and the costs of other commodities both publicly and privately provided. The demand for any particular good reflects the consumer's evaluation of that good in relation to all other ways in which his limited income could be used to yield satisfaction. If known, these individual household demands can be summed to derive the demand of the entire community for the social good. What must be added, however, is the amount that each family would pay for a given quantity of the public service. This quantity would be available free of direct charge to all persons in the community. That is, if family A is willing to pay $50 per year for a one-acre community park and family B will pay $100 for the same one-acre park, then the total demand for a one-acre park would be $150.

The economically efficient number of units of a social good is the quantity at which the total amount all households are willing to pay is equal to the cost. For each household the proper tax levy is equivalent to the amount it is willing to pay for the equilibrium number of units provided. Thus, households pay different amounts for a commonly provided number of units of social goods, and the variations in charges correspond to differences in benefits received. Taxation under the benefit principle equates for each household its monetary valuation of the last unit of a social good provided and the amount of tax paid. The ideal benefit solution to the provision of goods and services via the budget principle is essentially similar to the solution of the provision of goods and services under the market principle. In both situations the consumer equates his subjective valuation of the last unit taken to the price or tax he must pay to obtain that unit.

In practice, taxes to finance social goods are levied according to criteria that measure benefits imperfectly because it is impossible to assign the benefits of social goods to particular individuals. Furthermore, levels of expenditures for public goods are determined not by consumers' preferences manifested by willingness to pay but rather through a complex political process in which consumer preferences for social goods are many stages removed from the direct influence they exert over goods provided under the market principle.[3]

---

[3] See *ibid.*, Chapter 6, for an introduction to the problems of determining preferences for social goods by the political process. R. A. Dahl and C. E.

Production under Decreasing-Cost Conditions. In addition to government provision of goods and services with a collective or quasi-collective character there is another important reason for governmentally provided commodities. If a production process is such that the average cost of a commodity or service declines throughout the range of output which satisfies demand, private production will be inefficient. This situation, called "decreasing cost," results when a large quantity of fixed facilities is necessary to provide a service, but little additional expense is incurred to accommodate incremental users once the facility is in existence. The classic illustration of decreasing cost is the use of a bridge at rates within its engineering capacity. The crossing of an additional car (the marginal cost) adds imperceptibly to total costs but reduces average cost because total costs including construction costs are divided by an additional unit. A private producer would have to charge each car a price at least equal to the average cost per car if he wished to avoid losses. But the amount of socially useful resources used up by an extra car crossing the bridge is equal to the marginal cost. Charging a price equal to average cost instead of marginal cost will restrict the use of the facility to those whose valuation of benefits received is equal to the average cost instead of the marginal cost which is the proper measure of the value of the additional resources used.[4]

To prevent inadequate use of facilities where decreasing costs are persistent, two governmental policies are available. One is governmental provision free or at a price equal to marginal cost, and the use of tax proceeds to fill the gap between revenues and costs. The other is to provide subsidies to private producers to enable them to cover their costs and earn normal profits while charging prices that approximate their marginal rather than average costs.

This problem would not be nearly so severe if the facility involved were perfectly divisible and could readily be adjusted to a scale such that the demand curve always intersects the lowest point of the average cost curve. This is the scale toward which private productive facilities tend under competition. It is, however, usually impossible to know in advance the use of facilities such as bridges and waterways, and even once rates of use are known only gross adaptations of the original scale of such facilities are technologically possible.

Lindblom, *Politics, Economics, and Welfare* (New York: Harper & Brothers, 1953) is largely concerned with this issue.

[4] Bowen, *op. cit.*, Chapter 17 develops the decreasing-cost case in more detail.

It is common to find publicly provided goods and services partaking of both collective and decreasing cost characteristics. A public school may provide benefits to persons who never enter it, and at the same time the marginal cost of an additional pupil may be less than the average cost. Each of these elements alone, however, can be a sufficient reason for public provision. Even if the benefits from the school accrued only to those using it, a private operation making full charges would set the price above a socially desirable level if average cost exceeded marginal cost. On the other hand, even if additional pupils add proportionately to costs so that average and marginal costs are equal, the external benefits of education are large enough to dictate public provision.

Redistribution of Income. The market economy distributes shares of the total product according to the quantity of productive factors provided and the prices of these factors. Households possessing large amounts of scarce factors useful in producing products highly demanded by consumers will have high incomes, and be in a position to acquire substantial command over the social product. On the other hand, those owning few resources, less scarce and less productive, earn less and can obtain only small quantities of product. The explanation for the unequal distribution of factor endowments in the population lies partly in variations in human capacities and effort. Also, during the development of an economy certain groups acquire wealth and economic power and privileges which enable them to accumulate large amounts of land and capital to the benefit of their descendants.

In a market economy, allocating shares of the final product according to earned income, no matter how unequally distributed, provides the motive for owners of scarce factors to use them in their most socially productive way. Still, the resulting extremes in inequality are at variance with the standards of equity held today by most people throughout the world.

Altruism, however, is not the only reason for advocating the reduction of income inequality. In a rapidly changing economy the specific machinery and skills needed for production change quickly. Factor owners who were induced by high returns to specialize in particular areas may later find the economy demanding different labor skills and kinds of capital goods. Social justice requires some income subsidies to those whose previous responsiveness to economic forces leaves them presently in difficulties. Such subsidies may develop new vocational skills and encourage migration to new employment opportunities. Another reason for redistribution, less generally accepted today than during the early postdepression years, is that a substantial increase in aggregate expenditure will result if income is taken from those who save large portions and given to those who can be expected to spend all of it.

In the United States, as in other market-dominated economies, the government acts to moderate the extent of economic inequality. The goal of governmental policies in this area can be described as guaranteeing an adequate standard of living for all citizens by means of public programs which at the same time do not seriously impair work incentives or adjustments to changing economic conditions.

The relation between income redistribution and work incentives has received much attention. Receiving an income redistribution payment may reduce the number of hours workers choose to work because given levels of living can be achieved for fewer hours of work. This potential effect of income redistribution must not be overemphasized, however; not only are working hours largely institutionally determined, but a taste of higher levels of consumption made possible by income redistribution may raise workers' preferences for income over leisure and thereby cause them to work more rather than less. On the other hand, unemployment compensation may have some undesirable effects if it reduces workers' incentives to look for other employment. Labor mobility, however, can be excessive as well as inadequate. Economic efficiency is seldom promoted by the dissolution of a work force in response to a temporary lay-off because workers need immediately to find new jobs. Although the effects on incentives must be among the criteria for evaluating a redistribution program, a consideration of the issues shows that it is entirely unreasonable to use incentive arguments to rule out any income redistribution.

Although there is widespread popular support for income redistribution in the United States there is little agreement regarding the extent of redistribution or specific public policies for its achievement. There is substantial agreement that government should act to reduce sharply the inequalities in income resulting from monopolistic elements and from the improper use of other kinds of economic power. Antitrust laws, legislation against discrimination in employment, and legal arrangements equalizing bargaining power between labor and employers all tend to reduce income inequality by eliminating economic returns based on economic power and privilege rather than on contribution to production. Policies such as these which reduce concentrations of economic power and encourage social and economic mobility have not yet succeeded in reducing income inequality to levels acceptable to the general public. But considerable controversy remains with regard to the two major methods for further redistribution of income.

Those most strongly attached to the principles of consumer sovereignty advocate that socially desired levels of money income distribution should be achieved through outright transfers of income. Examples of such transfers include unemployment compensation and welfare payments to the aged and to families without breadwinners. The chief advantage of this method is that it retains the consumer-directed use of economic resources because the recipients of the income transfers use them as they choose. Opposed to this view is the notion that remedying the position of low-income families requires restructuring their consumption patterns so that they or their children will perform more effectively in the economic system. Income redistribution, under this arrangement, may involve some direct income transfers, but it stresses provision of free or highly subsidized housing, food staples, education, and other kinds of goods and services deemed desirable. The interference in consumer choice is defended on the grounds that direct income transfers would be squandered and would not contribute to the rehabilitation of the family. John K. Galbraith supports this approach when he writes that   *equality approach*

... we should invest more than proportionately in the children of the poor community. It is there that high quality schools, strong health services, special provision for nutrition and recreation are most needed to compensate for the very low investment which families are able to make in their own offspring. The effect of educational and related investment in individuals is to enable them to contend more effectively with their environment, to escape it and take up life elsewhere on more or less equal terms with others.[5]

The principles underlying the role of government in income redistribution are clear-cut; the extent of redistribution and the proper balance between income transfers and direct provision of free goods and services are, however, far from clear. Strong tradition, a concern for economic efficiency, and an awareness of demoralizing effects of state interference in personal behavior argue for a system of income transfers. However, when evidence strongly indicates that a family or group of families cannot or will not make sensible use of income transfers there is strong reason for redistribution through free goods.

Economic Stability and Growth. Economics is not only concerned

[5] John K. Galbraith, *The Affluent Society* (Boston: Houghton Mifflin Company, 1958), 330-31.

with the allocation of scarce resources and achieving an equitable distribution of income; in fact, most contemporary economic concern involves the broad over-all issues of maintaining full employment, avoiding inflation, and achieving adequate rates of economic growth. It has always been apparent that the sum of the myriad interrelated activities of a market economy can, at times, fail to add up to a properly functioning whole. Only in the last thirty years, however, have economists reached general agreement that conditions such as unemployment and inflation are not necessarily self-correcting and that concerted government action may be necessary to stabilize the economy. Even today there remains disagreement about the appropriateness, timing, and extent of various public policies for promoting economic stability.

The interrelated problems of full employment, price level stability, and economic growth are essentially questions of the relationship between the total potential production of the economy and the total demand for products by consumers, business firms, and governments. Total possible production or, as it is usually called, full employment output, is determined by the quantity of productive factors available for use, existing techniques of production, and the extent to which factor owners wish to use their factors. Consumer demand for products is primarily determined by consumer incomes. Business demand for final products takes the form of capital goods, such as new machines and buildings, and depends largely upon retained earnings and businessmen's expectations about the profitability of future production. Government demand stems from the need for employees and goods to provide public services.

When total demand is equal to total potential production all factors seeking employment at going rates of pay are employed, the quantity of goods produced is equal to the quantity demanded, and prices tend to remain steady. Further, if business spending exceeds the quantity of capital goods used up in the year's production, the amount of plant and equipment in existence increases and potential production in the next year grows because other factors have more physical capital with which to work. If aggregate spending is less than potential production some factors will not be needed to provide for the low level of demand, and in the adjustment to this lower level of production excess supplies of products, plant capacities, and workers will tend to reduce the over-all level of prices. In these circumstances businessmen may become pessimistic about the future and reduce their demand for capital goods. A further cumulative decline in demand may result in which there is widespread unemployment, further falling of prices, and little new capital formation. When aggregate demand exceeds potential production, businessmen, consumers, and governments vie for an insufficient quantity of output and thereby push prices up and stimulate capital goods formation. Rising commodity prices impose hardships on those with relatively fixed incomes, and increasing costs of production create uncertainty about prospects for future profits and depress business spending. More and more economic activity turns away from production and toward speculation and other ways of making capital gains.

If the discrepancy between full employment production and aggregate demand is small and the cause transitory, the self-regulating aspects of a market economy may restore the balance. When the difference is substantial and is a consequence of a persistent influence, market forces are likely to be inadequate, and failure to take early action can lead to deep and prolonged depression or ruinous inflation. Governmental policies to prevent such destabilizing swings of the over-all economy aim at balancing aggregate demand and total production. In addition, if full employment at relatively stable prices is maintained, businessmen's expectations will be conducive to capital formation, and adequate rates of economic growth encouraged.

Two major governmental policies for influencing aggregate demand are available. In one, fiscal policy, governmental expenditures and taxes are varied so that the contribution to total demand made by government ensures the proper level of aggregate demand. If demand is to be stimulated, taxes can be reduced raising consumer incomes and thereby increasing their spending, or government expenditures on goods and services can be increased which directly raises total demand. Other possible budgetary actions include government transfer payments to individuals, similar in effect to tax reductions, and even increased government spending out of equally increased tax receipts, which will have an over-all stimulating effect. Demand can be decreased through fiscal policy by reversing the direction of the tax and expenditure adjustments.

In monetary policy, the second technique, government acts to influence the cost of borrowing to business firms. Since many business purchases of capital goods are financed by borrowing, an increase in these costs will make prospective investment less profitable and depress business spending, while a decrease can be expected to stimulate business demand. Monetary policy can be effective, however, only to the extent that interest costs or the availability of funds is a determining factor in business investment policies. If deficiencies in anticipated demand outweigh the lower costs of borrowing in periods of depression and alternative sources of funds can be tapped in periods of "tight money," monetary policy will not be sufficiently effective in influencing business spending.

The simple principles of stabilization policy presented above have been highly developed and refined to deal with particular aspects of economic stabilization. Today's dynamic economy requires differentiating between general deficiencies in aggregate demand, and structural discrepancies in demand and supply in particular segments of the economy where adjustments have not yet been made to changing patterns of economic activity. Further, rapidly shifting economic conditions make the proper timing of stabilization policies most difficult. The refinements cannot be developed here, but one point regarding variations in public expenditures on goods and services as a stabilizing device is especially relevant to educational spending.

Varying public outlays for goods and services with fixed levels of taxation changes aggregate spending in the same direction as the shift in expenditures. Similar changes in aggregate demand can be achieved by manipulating taxes or government transfer payments. Is there any reason for preferring one method to another? A concern for the efficient use of economic resources indicates that tax and transfer payments should be used to influence aggregate demand. Levels of resource using public expenditure should be determined in response to public demand for the services provided by governmental bodies and variations in such expenditures should occur only when public demand changes. When aggregate demand is increased in the interest of economic stabilization, the increased spending should be for those commodities, private and public, which consumers most desire and not necessarily for public works or other public services. This approach requires that governments place in the hands of consumers adequate purchasing power to insure proper amounts of aggregate demand and enact policies which achieve an equitable distribution of this income. Consumers then decide whether they want more private goods, by using their income to buy them, or more public goods, by voting for increased public spending or for representatives who advocate such spending. The argument is parallel in considering a reduction of aggregate demand. Public projects should not be reduced automatically as a method of lowering excessive demand. Rather, incomes of consumers ought to be reduced by raising taxes and cutting back transfer payments, and the proper balance between private and public resource use achieved on the basis of consumer preferences.

Aside from the considerable problems of adjusting public projects to changing consumer preferences, the efficiency argument against variations in public works as a component of stabilization policy is valid only if existing public projects are of proper magnitude. If the process for converting consumer preferences for public projects into actual governmental expenditures inadequately reflects these preferences, the general level of such projects will be too low. It is argued by many that present levels of public expenditure in the United States are inadequate and that increased public use of resources would yield benefits in excess of the returns obtained from their present private use.[6] If this is true, stabilization policy involving increased public works would move the economy toward a more efficient use of its resources. At the same time, curtailment of public projects because of inflationary tendencies in the economy is always inappropriate except in the unlikely situation where public projects are excessive in terms of consumer choice.

This discussion of public expenditures in a market-guided economy has emphasized three reasons for government spending: to provide goods and services not adequately provided by the market, to achieve a more equitable distribution of the total product, and to stabilize the over-all economy. Expenditures for a particular purpose may contribute to all of these objectives. Spending for public education, for example, provides a service which would be insufficiently provided privately, redistributes income by giving education to many families who pay few or no taxes, and the increase in total demand for goods may occur when aggregate demand is insufficient.

THE LEVEL OF GOVERNMENT AND PUBLIC EXPENDITURES

Although all levels of government in the United States have the power to undertake public expenditures, differences in the extent of area governed as well as constitutional limitations in taxing, borrowing, and money-creating capacities circumscribe the expenditure functions undertaken by each level of government.[7]

The federal government must provide those public services whose

---

[6] Galbraith, *ibid.*, strongly argues that the public sector in the United States is undernourished.

[7] A conservative discussion of the responsibilities of various levels of government in the United States is found in the Commission on Intergovernmental Relations, *A Report to the President* (Washington, 1955). The views of several economists on this subject are presented in *Federal Expenditure Policy for Growth and Stability* (Washington: Joint Economic Committee, 1957), 85-162.

benefits accrue to persons located throughout the nation. Thus, national defense, regional conservation, and similar services are the domain of the central government. In addition, economic stabilization, which at times requires deficits of several billion dollars and which aims at influencing large segments of the nation's economy, is the province of the federal government. Finally, redistribution among geographical regions can be performed only by the central level of government.

State governments are in a position to redistribute income among areas and among individuals within the state. States also provide public services such as highway construction and maintenance, higher education, recreation, and some social welfare services primarily benefiting state residents.

Local governments are largely responsible for providing public services whose benefits are usually confined to persons residing within or near the boundaries of the governmental unit. Cities, towns, counties, school districts, and special districts spend for local roads, education, police and fire protection, recreation, sanitation, and similar functions. Most locally performed public functions require minimum service levels for successful operation and often local governments have inadequate taxing powers to raise these necessary revenues. Other local governments may have far more taxpaying capacity than needed for minimum standards of service. But, because local governments are thought to be more aware of the desires of their residents and more capable of evaluating the consequences of public spending, they continue to have major responsibilities for local public services even though the requisites of effective tax administration prevent them from using taxes commensurate with their expenditure obligations. This difficulty is remedied in part through grants-in-aid from the states and to a lesser degree from the federal government. These grants may be redistributive or may merely represent the repayment of taxes collected by the state in the local area.

Despite a trend toward increasing state and federal grants-in-aid to local units of government these transfers have not kept pace, relatively, with local government spending. Students of public finance and political science are not agreed on the proper role for state and federal grants-in-aid to localities. Taxes and grants for regional redistribution clearly are the province of higher governmental levels. Considerations of tax administration favor state and federal tax collections and reimbursement to local governments. Against lower collection costs and the ability to use the more equitable personal income tax must be set reduced local autonomy over types of taxes and tax rates which generally but not necessarily result. When a moderate portion of the benefits from the provision of a service by a local government extends to residents of other areas within the state or to those living outside the state, then outright state and federal contributions to expenditures should be added to local funds. If the benefits accrue to virtually all residents of the state or nation without regard for locale, the service should be undertaken as a state or federal function. However, to secure state and federal grants local governments must often provide matching funds. This requirement influences the pattern of local spending and is intended to increase the total amount spent for the function for which matched moneys are provided, although spending of local funds may be reduced. Alterations in the mix of local government services are desirable if the matching grant changes the relative costs of services to take all benefits into account. It is an undesirable distortion, however, if the grant is applied to functions whose full benefits would be taken into account in local government decisions in the absence of such grants.

ECONOMIC ASPECTS OF EXPENDITURES FOR EDUCATION

A complete theory of expenditures for public education, in the context of a consumer-directed market economy, must explain several aspects of educational spending. The theory should provide a framework for determining whether educational services should be produced privately or publicly. It must suggest, on the basis of a concern for proper allocation of resources, redistribution of income, and economic stabilization, the proper amount of governmental contributions for educational outlays, and the pattern of taxes for raising these revenues. Finally, if education is to be publicly produced as well as financed, the theory must indicate which level of government is to be responsible for its production.

It is crucial to recognize that this discussion of optimum expenditures for education is for a consumer-directed economy in which the rate of economic growth is determined primarily by individual preferences for saving and expectations about the returns to investment. There is today great interest in education as a means to increase the rate of economic development; in systems where the rate of economic growth is planned, rather than left largely to the result of individual decisions, educational outlays are based on anticipated contributions to development.

Under these circumstances expenditures for education are calculated by the application of cost figures to estimates of the

educational needs that underlie manpower and other requirements
of the plan. In this study, however, it is assumed that individual
preferences direct the operation of the economy and determine the
rate of economic growth. As a result, there is no discussion of an
optimum educational program based on an economic plan. There is a
role for educational planning in market economies, but such planning
is largely concerned with the estimation of the amount and kind of
educational facilities which will be demanded in the future on the
basis of anticipated labor force requirements, rates of pay, and
educational costs. There is no attempt to determine what educational
requirements are necessary to achieve a given rate of growth, but
rather an attempt to specify what educational facilities will be
demanded in the view of the expected "natural" growth of the
economy.

Public Versus Private School Operation

The controversy over whether the provision of elementary and
secondary education should be by private or public schools is different
from the question of public or private financing of education. A system
of public financing of education by subsidies to private schools or by
transfer payments to families for tuition payments to private schools
embodies government financing and private production. Government
contracts with private firms to provide school services would also
involve private production and public finance.

The economic issues involved in the choice between public or
private operation of schools are efficiency, equity, and conformity
with consumer preferences. With regard to efficiency the question is,
simply, whether public or private provision of given levels of educational services is less costly. Publicly operated school systems,
attended by the great majority of pupils in an area, are more likely
to attain a scale of operation which provides an opportunity for ideal
specialization in instruction and administration. Thus, they are in a
position to provide given levels of education at lowest cost. Against
the benefits of achieving optimum size there is the argument that
private operation of schools would introduce the profit motive and
thereby provide an incentive for an efficiently run school system. The
dedication to cost reduction on the part of public school administrators
is legend throughout the United States. However, even if private
operation, in its search for profits, would offset the economies of
scale of public schools, this very search for profits must give rise to
serious concern about private operation of publicly supported education.

Those who advocate private operation contend that major benefits lie in providing a greater number of alternative educational products. The consumer can choose the type of school he most desires in view of his income and attitudes about education. A relatively large number of private schools will be operating in an area, providing different kinds of education at different prices, and each will be competing for the parents' dollars, some of which will be provided by government grants to parents to be used for educational purposes.[8]

An entrepreneur producing for profit will try to provide the school which has the greatest appeal to parents. But most parents are not experts on education, and unlike the consumption of many privately produced goods, the consequences of an education cannot be appraised after a brief exposure—especially since it is the child, not the parent, who is getting the education. Competition may also produce sameness, not variation, in educational offerings. Further, the appropriateness of an education depends to a considerable degree on the characteristics of future society, and here again parents are not likely to possess the knowledge for a wise choice. A private system permits parents to decide how much above the amount provided by government is to be spent for a youngster's education. But differences in income, occupation, educational attainment of parents, and other economic, social, and cultural factors will determine the amount spent. It seems likely that the social structure will be made more rigid by such an arrangement for education. At the same time, parents with strong desires for upward mobility for their children may try to project them into upper social strata by placing them in the more expensive schools, although it is not certain that such attempts to rise in the social hierarchy will be successful. More importantly, it would give those who prefer a higher level or different kind of education than that provided by a community with its single public school system a more equitable opportunity to effectuate their preferences. The present system of publicly operated as well as financed schools has been criticized because it imposes on those who choose nonpublic education for their children the dual burden of a contribution to taxation for public education and tuition to a private school.

Public education does not provide the freedom of choice of a variegated set of private schools. However, to the extent that a parent is free to choose his place of residence, he may be able to choose

---

[8] A carefully reasoned argument for such a scheme is Milton Friedman, "The Role of Government in Education," Robert A. Solo, ed., *Economics and the Public Interest* (New Brunswick: Rutgers University Press, 1955), 123-44.

among several school systems offering various educational programs and tax structures.[9] For most families other factors determining selection of residence, many more compelling than the character of the educational services available, greatly limit this freedom. Instead of a range of choices, public education provides to all who desire it free common education based, roughly, on educational concepts developed by a profession devoted to elementary and secondary education. Educational administrators, and the politically determined budget within which they operate, establish the kind of education provided. For those attending public schools, the character of the education received is not supposed to depend directly on parental income, preferences, or other similar circumstances. Consumer sovereignty is bypassed except insofar as it influences political behavior and local organizations such as parent-teacher associations. But, income inequality, imperfect knowledge of parents, inappropriate parental attitudes in determining the future of children, all call for interfering with consumer sovereignty in education.

Public conduct, or to use Friedman's term, "nationalization," of elementary and secondary education imposes the community's view of proper education on all but those wealthy enough to pay their taxes and still afford private schools. By using standards determined by professional educators, the community substitutes a consensus of experts for individual judgments. In so doing it curtails individual choice, perhaps reduces total educational outlay, and diminishes the diversity of educational backgrounds. At the same time public schools promote social mobility and equality of opportunity. They turn a most crucial decision in a child's life from a private family matter to a public concern. So long as great disparities exist among families' capacities and desires for education for their children a social decision seems appropriate. There are gains from public education for those whose families would, under a market system, choose inadequate education or be forced by financial, racial, or social status to utilize "second-class" private schools. These gains appear greatly to outweigh the losses resulting from the partially curtailed freedom of choice of those relatively few whose economic and social situation would permit a wide range of private educational alternatives.[10]

---

[9] The notion that in selecting a place to live a family can achieve a degree of choice in public service levels similar to the choice among private goods is developed in Charles M. Tiebout, "A Pure Theory of Local Expenditures," LXIV *Journal of Political Economy* (October 1956), 416-24.

[10] See the illuminating discussions of the question of public versus private operation of schools in Charles S. Benson, *The Economics of Public Education*

Optimum Amounts of Public Spending and Taxation for Education

Equating Benefits and Costs. A strict application of the principles of economic efficiency would set the level of educational spending at a point where the benefits of additional spending were just equal to the burdens of the necessary taxation. The equating of benefits and costs (taxes) would be achieved for each individual and business which used educational services. In this view the benefits of education are reflected in the willingness of households and business firms to pay for various levels of elementary and secondary education provided in a community. [Burdens are measured by the value to households of the increased consumption and saving they could have obtained from the funds taxed away for educational expenditures.]

Household demands for education are based on the value of educational services to the pupil or his family. These demands reflect desires of parents for education so that their children's lifetime earnings will be higher,[11] or simply because they believe education will heighten the children's enjoyment of life. Household demand for education also encompasses the value of education to persons unrelated to pupils who find satisfaction in the education of others because of the cultural, political, and interpersonal characteristics of an educated society. Derived demand for education by producers, similar to their demand for productive inputs, is an additional component of the total demand for education. Increased outlay for education in a community provides a more productive work force, and so long as the value of the increased output due to greater educational skills of the workers exceeds the cost of additional educational services, the producers stand to gain from increased outlay. A summation of producers' derived demand plus consumers' final and derived demand comprises the total demand for educational spending.[12] Theoretically, where total demand is equal to the unit cost of goods or services an economically efficient level of output is achieved.

(Boston: Houghton Mifflin Company, 1961), 320-32, and John Vaizey, *The Economics of Education* (New York: The Free Press of Glencoe Inc., 1962), 26-36.

[11] The nature of this demand is similar to the derived demand for education by producers described later in this paragraph.

[12] To the extent that increased productivity by workers is reflected in higher wages, producers' demand for education will be a reflection of workers' demand. Clearly, such demand must be counted only once. However, increased productivity in one area of production due to education reduces costs of production in other related areas without raising wages. The reflection of this element of gain from education is a separate producer demand, and therefore must be added to workers' demand.

There is one aspect of education that makes it appear that the cost of education is greater than the teachers' services, books, buildings, and other resources used up in the production of education. Theodore Schultz and others engaged in the estimation of the costs of education in the United States argue that total costs also must include earnings foregone because students were attending school rather than working.[13] For pupils in secondary grades and those in institutions of higher education this opportunity cost has been estimated as approximately equal to actual monetary outlays. The conceptual propriety of this treatment of earnings foregone as an element in the cost of education is not agreed upon by all economists, and in the United States compulsory education laws and requirements regarding minimum age for work reduce greatly the importance of earnings foregone as a cost factor in elementary and secondary education. However, especially for the last few years of secondary school, some of the hours spent at school would otherwise have been spent at work, and, consequently, there are earnings and products foregone. The implications for the equation of benefits and costs is that where there are earnings foregone, the cost of education is greater than the burden of the taxation to provide the necessary funds. Thus, given the benefits of education, the optimum level of expenditure is lower than it would be if earnings foregone were ignored.

Effects on Production. Another problem in the determination of the total demand for education arises because educational attainments often yield scientific, administrative, and other cost-reducing discoveries. The original discoverers or their employers can, for a short time, obtain an economic gain from the sale of their uniquely productive innovation. After a while the innovation becomes known and unless it is the kind of discovery that can be patented it is used by other producers to lower their costs. This development is highly desirable from society's standpoint because it enables the economy to provide more product out of its limited resources. But the original discoverer is unable to gain an economic payment for the further use of his discovery. Realizing this, his demand for education, or his employer's demand for education for him, will be limited by that portion of the increased product that can be privately captured. The further social gains of widespread use will not appear as part of any private demand for education because it cannot be privately captured. As a result, the economically correct level of derived demand for

---

[13] Theodore W. Schultz, "Capital Formation by Education," LXVIII *Journal of Political Economy* (December 1960), 571-83.

education by producers should include the indirect cost-reducing effects of increased levels of education which increase the productivity of other producers.

The effects of one producer's behavior on the costs of production of other producers, called "external effects" or "external economies," occur over time as well as at a given moment. Increased educational outlays which raise productivity make higher rates of economic growth possible.[14] Growth may be more rapid because an increased product can provide more capital goods (i.e., buildings, machines) while consumption remains unchanged or rises by less than the increase in productivity. However, most of the gains from more rapid economic growth will be enjoyed by future generations whose preferences exert no influence on the current use of economic resources. Market-determined outlays for education, therefore, will not adequately reflect the value to future generations of the contribution to economic growth from contemporary levels of spending for elementary and secondary education. Here the private approach to education fails to register the social demand of future generations.

The complex nature of the total demand for education is a result of the many economic effects of education that cannot be captured through a market transaction because they accrue to others besides the student. A market solution to the output of goods or services is an ideal one only when private or personal benefits and costs are the sole significant elements. Private demand for education does not reflect satisfactions gained by individuals other than students and cost reductions for firms other than those whose employees receive education. Since the market fails to register these consequences the amount of education supplied is inadequate. Theoretically, the economist can say that the total demand, including private and nonprivate elements, should determine educational outlays. The virtual impossibility of determining the magnitude of these public elements renders the concept of an educational optimum nonoperational.

A level of educational spending consistent with private and nonprivate consumer and producer demand, even if attained, still would not necessarily be an optimum from an economic standpoint. The relationships between levels of public education and income distri-

---

[14] For discussions of the relationship of education and economic growth see Theodore W. Schultz, "Investment in Human Capital," LI *The American Economic Review* (March 1961), 1-17; Vaizey, *op. cit.*, 37-53; and Edward F. Denison, *The Sources of Economic Growth in the United States and the Alternatives Before Us* (New York: Committee for Economic Development, 1962), 67-79.

bution and economic stability are also involved in the determination of educational spending.

Income Redistribution and Public Education. Educational outlays in excess of the amounts demanded by individuals and business firms may be undertaken as an income redistribution technique. Families with low incomes are not likely to demand heavy educational outlays, but the community may decide that increased educational services should be consumed by children in such families. As a way of redistributing income and controlling the use of the extra income, additional education is provided without assessing extra tax liabilities on low-income families.

As was argued above, the issue here is whether the recipient should decide on the disposition of redistributed income. When the shortcomings of consumer sovereignty in determining a family's outlay for education are taken into account, there is no clear economic answer to this problem. Supporters of the market economy emphasize the social and cultural values of freedom of choice, but few would dissent from the proposition that a necessary step in breaking the chain of successive generations of poverty and lack of motivation is satisfactory elementary and secondary education for children. Especially where the future of children is at stake, a doctrinaire adherence to the principles of consumer sovereignty by policymakers may doom still another generation to a marginal life economically, socially, and culturally.

Economic Stabilization and Educational Outlays. Educational spending to promote economic stability is not consistent with contemporary theories of controlling business cycles, although increased educational outlays have been proposed as antirecessionary measures. Plans for new school buildings could be kept in readiness and implemented when there were indications of unemployment. Also, increases in teaching staffs and other components of current expenditures could occur when economic conditions warranted increased public spending.

A broader view is that educational outlays are justified by their economic, social, political, and other benefits and, therefore, adequate levels of public education should be provided regardless of the desirability of governmental expenditures for stabilization purposes. Stabilization policy should aim at providing full employment, stable prices, and adequate rates of economic growth, and in so doing must take into account the level of demand for goods and services produced by governments. The determination of the quantity of public services to be provided should, in turn, be based on an appraisal of needs and desires for such services assuming that stabilization policies achieve full employment. If stabilization aims are confused with supplying the proper amounts of public goods and services, resources will not be used where they yield the greatest benefits.

Educational Spending by Different Levels of Government

The concept of an ideal division of responsibility among the various government levels for financing and providing public elementary and secondary education has been much discussed. From an economic point of view, one aspect of the issue is to allocate responsibility so that final and derived demands for education are reflected in the total amount of educational spending while, at the same time, tax burdens are assessed in relation to benefits received. Insofar as income in the form of education is preferred to transfer payments as a redistributive technique, further educational outlays must be provided without assessing taxes in accordance with benefits. In addition, government responsibilities should be distributed so as to minimize the costs of educational services as well as the costs of tax collection. In the context of the present federal system in the United States, such objectives imply the involvement of all levels of government in financing public education.

Local Government. At the local level governments are most capable of adapting the quantity of spending and the character of the public school system to the demands of those directly using the schools and to the business firms and individuals who will be most immediately affected by the nature of elementary and secondary schools. The dominance of local governments in operating public schools in the United States today is largely the consequence of these circumstances. However, only a portion of total educational spending should be locally determined and financed. Benefits accruing to persons and business firms outside the boundaries of the local government must also be reflected in educational revenues and expenditures for local pupils. Also, local taxes are unlikely to be redistributive even within the local community; redistribution across regions requires state and federal participation. Further, even though expenditures are under local control, local revenue systems may not be capable of effective tax administration and state and federal taxation may be a superior way of raising revenues from residents for education. The widespread benefits of education and problems of local tax administration require the participation of state and federal governments in educational finance.

Granting an important place to local government in financing and administering public schools still leaves unresolved one of the most controversial aspects of public school government in the United States: the question of whether school systems should be fiscally dependent or independent. A fiscally independent local school district has delegated to its officers by a mandate of the state the powers of authorizing taxation and expenditures for public education within its boundaries. In contrast, in a fiscally dependent system, a government unit, such as a municipality or county, has responsibility for various public functions including the determination of the budget for education.

The choice between these two fiscal arrangements involves far-ranging issues of control, curriculum, professional standards, and finance. The crucial economic question is which system is better able to weigh the benefits of alternative uses of public funds and the burdens of increased taxation and implement these choices through a public budget. In addition, economic considerations favor the arrangement which provides a given educational program at least cost.

In principle, fiscal dependence clearly is superior in its capacity for including competing claims for scarce resources in the governmental decision-making process. Those who argue that fiscal independence should be preferred because it takes politics out of the determination of educational spending fail to recognize that government expenditures are intended to be politically determined. In fact, fiscal independence does not remove decisions from politics but forces them into a political mold which is unduly inflexible and unresponsive to the full range of public needs and resources.[15] Unfortunately, present political arrangements and budgetary procedures in fiscally dependent systems also do not provide great opportunity for the revelation and implementation of individual preferences nor for a comparison of the returns to alternative local government expenditures.

Economic arguments for fiscal independence emphasize the unique attributes of public education in recruiting and retaining staff, in the size of expenditure, and in the desirability of local control of educational spending. Placing the power over educational budgets in a local government which is responsible for multiple functions does not remove local control, but rather makes local control of educational

15 Julius Margolis, "Metropolitan Finance Problems: Territories, Functions, and Growth," in *Public Finances: Needs, Sources, and Utilization* (Princeton: National Bureau of Economic Research, 1961), 241-44 and 260-61, makes a strong argument for fiscal dependence throughout the metropolitan area as a strategy for providing more funds for all public purposes.

outlays a part of local control of all locally provided public services. Furthermore, centralization of hiring, purchasing, and other aspects of governmental administration may lower costs.

The ultimate concern to the public finance economist is the effectiveness with which resources are used in the public sector. From this standpoint fiscally dependent school districts appear more appropriate.[16] If, however, evidence reveals that the political process in cities and counties which control school budgets consistently provides fewer resources to public education than appears warranted, the case for fiscal dependence is greatly weakened. The social issue is not which arrangement results in the largest expenditures for local education, but which achieves the best balance in the over-all use of resources for public purposes.

State Government. There are three dominant economic reasons for state government participation in public education. One is to represent geographic external or "spill-over" benefits of education. Another is to promote intrastate income redistribution by providing education without commensurate tax burdens to low-income families. Finally, states collect tax revenues from residents and business firms in local communities by the administratively more efficient state tax system and then return these funds through grants to the local governments in which the revenues originated.

Much more extensive state participation would be justified if state operation of local public schools resulted in substantially reduced costs, although the success of school district consolidation programs in recent years has greatly reduced the number of inefficiently small school systems. While considerably more consolidation is needed in a few states, there appears to be no necessity for actual state operation to achieve economically sized school systems. State operation might, however, provide strong incentive for educational research and experimentation which individual local school systems now find hardly worthwhile. Under local control state-sponsored research can still be undertaken, and states can act as purchasing agents and guarantors of credit for local schools. Further, if states are not to abandon concern for differences in local community attitudes toward education, they must allow local variations in educational spending and services. It appears, then, that states can best reduce educational costs by promoting consolidations, by engaging in and supporting basic research on educational methods, and by using the financial strength

---

[16] Benson, *op. cit.*, 495, comes to the opposite conclusion on the basis of a consideration of the same arguments.

of the state to obtain the most favorable terms for local school purchases and bond issues.

Federal Government. The economic function of the federal government in financing local public schools rests on the nationwide benefits of education, the federal government's responsibility for regional redistribution of income, and the inherent advantages of a federally administered tax system. National benefits from education include the gains to individuals and businesses throughout the nation from education provided to pupils in local schools and benefits such as strengthened national defense, which cannot be assigned to individuals. To the extent that these nonmarket benefits cross state boundaries, and to the extent that people move from state to state, the central government alone can make such considerations effective in influencing educational outlays by granting to local school governments funds derived from the entire nation. Also, only the central government, through a system of taxation and grants, can redistribute income regionally and thereby modify the economic base out of which local school spending is derived.

A further economic task for the central government is use of the federal tax system to obtain revenues to be repaid to the localities taxed. An advantage of such a procedure is that the federal government can effectively employ more equitable taxes, such as the personal income tax, and greater reliance on federal taxation would lessen pressures for competitive tax concessions by state and local governments to induce industrial location. Also, instead of requiring the maintenance of the myriad of small tax-collection agencies that result when every local and state governmental unit collects taxes, the federal government is able to administer tax collections with a single central staff employing modern data processing and auditing techniques.

Structure of Governmental Responsibilities for Public School Finance. Within the argument developed here the local government is still left with several aspects of public school finance. Local governments operate the local schools and have the power, within standards set by the state, to hire staff, determine curriculum and length of school day and term, and perform other vital educational functions. In addition, local school governments determine the amount of locally collected revenue for education. It is likely that local taxes could be reduced and a more equitable local tax burden achieved if the state or federal tax system were used to obtain revenues for local governments. The implementation of such a plan requires a flexible set of "supplementary" tax rates which can be added to state and federal taxes and from which local governments could choose.

The ultimate general pattern of governmental responsibility that follows from these economic concerns is that local governments administer the schools and contribute toward total educational outlays an amount determined by the local communities' demand for education. The funds for these outlays should come from local residents and business firms according to acceptable standards of equitable burden although they may be raised by the state or even the federal tax system and returned to the point of collection. To this amount is added the demand for education emanating from benefits of education obtained by persons residing outside the locality. The funds for these outlays come from sources outside the local government. Finally, state and federal grants to local schools to redistribute income in the form of educational services provide additional sources of funds for educational spending by local systems.

In this chapter education is examined in the context of fundamental economic concepts regarding the allocation of resources, the distribution of income, economic stability and growth, and the economic functions of government. There are several key characteristics of education that determine the results of the analysis. Education is both consumption and investment. It provides direct and indirect satisfactions to those who receive educational services, and it also raises the productivity of labor by increasing human capacities for production. As consumption and investment, education is a social good because a considerable portion of the benefits of education accrues to persons other than the students themselves, and there is no way of capturing these external benefits through a market transaction. A good education can provide a means of escape from the cycle of poverty and lack of motivation that characterizes certain segments of society. Evaluating an educational program for one's children is not like buying a loaf of bread, and consumer (parent) sovereignty will not necessarily lead to the best choice.

Applying economic analysis to these characteristics of education leads to some definite conclusions. Because of the external benefits the appropriate allocation of resources to education requires that it be publicly financed and provided free of direct charge. Also, persons outside the local community should bear a portion of the costs of local schools. The crucial social consequences of education militate for income redistribution through taxation and provision of publicly operated education and against subsidized private operation of schools. Ability to pay must not be the primary determinant of individual consumption of elementary and secondary education. Local control of education has no clear-cut economic drawbacks and provides a close link between popular attitudes toward education and the thinking of the professional educator. Such control, however, should serve to make the choice among various local public programs as sharp as possible by making clear the benefits of each; it should not be a means for considering educational outlays in isolation.

III. Empirical Studies of the Determinants of Public Expenditures

THIS CHAPTER reviews the major studies of determinants of public spending. An examination of previous empirical work reveals regularities that have been discovered and illustrates alternative approaches and pitfalls. Such a review also provides a framework for the specific approach used in the statistical study of local school system expenditures, the details of which are described in the following two chapters.

REQUISITES OF A PREDICTIVE THEORY OF PUBLIC SPENDING

A positive theory that aims at explaining actual levels of public spending is quite different from the normative theory, described in Chapter II, that considers how much ought to be spent. The positive theory must identify each of the major determinants of public spending and estimate the direction and magnitude of its effect. In statistical terms, the variance of public expenditures must be accounted for by variations in certain independent variables. Also, if implications of cause and effect rather than associative relationships are to be drawn, a further requisite of a positive theory is that the distinction between dependent and independent variables be based on a logical, theoretical structure that explains the distinction.

Attempts to explain the determination of public spending, like most efforts to estimate empirical relationships between dependent and independent variables in the behavioral sciences, are complicated by two factors. First, empirical study of public expenditures cannot use experimental methods. Randomization, a procedure in which variations in the dependent variable are achieved by systematic variations in the independent variables, is the major device used in empirical study for segregating dependent from independent variables and for avoiding intercorrelation among independent variables. Obviously, it cannot be used in studying public spending or in most other investigations in the social sciences. Instead, a statistical model must be developed which uses nonexperimental data so that inferences similar to those resulting from the use of experimental data can be drawn. A second difficulty in dealing empirically with public spending is that no clear-cut operationally formulated theory has been developed which indicates the crucial independent variables whose effects are to be estimated by empirical study. In public spending, unlike private consumption, economists and other social scientists are just beginning analytic study of the factors associated with behavior.

A representation or depiction of the essential aspects of the underlying behaviors and interrelationships that determine the value of a dependent variable is frequently called a model. Particular models for empirical study of government outlays differ in many ways. Most fundamental are differences in the nature of the dependent variable to be explained. The study of expenditures for a particular purpose (e.g., highways) by a specific government (e.g., a city) is an atomistic approach. A bit more aggregative is the investigation of total spending by a specific level of government (e.g., cities, counties, states). Finally, there is the consideration of total expenditures for a particular purpose by all levels of government, and, most aggregative, the total of all public spending regardless of purpose or level of government.

Aggregative analysis of social phenomena is quite useful, but the "building-blocks" of the behavioral sciences are empirical models based on actual decision-making units. Since total expenditures arise from the actions of individual governments, an explanatory theory of public spending must rest ultimately on an understanding of how various factors influence public decision-making units. At the same time, those searching for regularities in government spending must explicitly recognize the interactions among governments, both at the same level and at different levels. A fully articulated theory of public expenditure would explain the expenditures of one government, not only as a result of conditions prevailing within its boundaries, but also as a consequence of expenditures by other governments. Such a system could only be solved simultaneously for all units. Furthermore, for full generality, this framework for determining public spending would have to be integrated with models for household and business behavior.[1]

Although such an ambitious model cannot be implemented, an examination of its implications is instructive for viewing actual studies of spending in the public sector. Given values for the independent variable, the ideal model would yield estimates of spending for all

[1] A description of such a model is found in Werner Z. Hirsch, "Interindustry Relations of a Metropolitan Area," XLI *Review of Economics and Statistics* (November 1959), 360-69.

purposes by each government during a period. Further, year-to-year changes in spending would be estimated on the basis of changes in the independent variables. The study of public expenditures is not sufficiently developed so that a single model can accomplish both of these tasks. Instead, specific approaches aim at explaining either differences in spending among governments at the same time or differences in spending by a government at different points in time. The approach that examines the same unit of government over successive periods of time is time-series analysis, and the study of different units at the same time is cross-sectional analysis. Although the variables that explain changes over time are likely to be similar to those used in cross-sectional studies that explain variations among different units in the same year, time series and cross-section relationships are different enough so that explanatory models and results will vary.

There is no single "correct" representation for predicting public spending in general or spending for education in particular. The nature of the model depends on the questions asked. In this monograph the major interest is in the theoretical and empirical reasons for variations in expenditures for elementary and secondary education by the various governments legally responsible for such expenditures. The empirical study described in the next chapter uses an atomistic, cross-section approach based on the fundamental decision-making unit. Some previous studies have used similar methods, while in others rather different techniques were employed. The remainder of this chapter is a critical review of the most important of these studies in the United States.[2]

ANALYTIC STUDIES OF TOTAL PUBLIC SPENDING

Early analyses of public spending were largely concerned with organizing data by levels of government and by expenditures for specific functions. When available, demographic and economic characteristics of the area were related to government expenditures. More powerful techniques for taking several determinants of expenditures into account simultaneously were not employed until the early 1940's. The brief review presented here concentrates on studies that aim at explaining public expenditures and, therefore, omit the important but preliminary work that primarily present and organize data.

[2] Studies of empirical determinants of public spending in countries other than the United States have been omitted from this review.

The hypothesis that public spending is subject to regularities and can be explained in terms of changing characteristics of a nation or of local governments is attributed to Adolph Wagner. Writing in 1892 Wagner concluded "that in the course of economic progress governmental budgets increase more than private business activities."[3] Over the years this general hypothesis on the behavior of government budgets has been extended to a search for the specific characteristics that influence public spending—a search made possible by the increased availability of data and the development of statistical techniques for estimating the magnitudes of multi-variate relationships.

Growth of Governmental Expenditures Over Time

The publication in 1952 of Solomon Fabricant's *Trend of Governmental Activity in the United States Since 1900* was a major contribution to the study of expenditures.[4] However, neither Fabricant nor others who have recently studied historical trends in government spending in the United States have attempted any systematic statistical estimation of the factors responsible for changes in total government spending or in total spending for particular functions.[5] Instead, they describe the factors believed to be important based on inspection of carefully assembled data. For example, Dewhurst and Associates, in their massive study of U.S. needs and resources, partition the causes of the increase in total governmental expenditures into price increases, population growth, and growth of service provided.[6] The method used, however, is a form of projection that does not explain to what extent particular changes in economic, demographic, and political characteristics influence the growth of spending.

Projections of total government spending and of spending for specific functions are made periodically by economists and others

[3] Quoted by Joseph Berolzheimer, "Influences Shaping Expenditures for Operation of State and Local Governments," XXXII *Bulletin of the National Tax Association* (March 1947), 170n.

[4] Solomon Fabricant, *The Trend of Government Activity in the United States since 1900* (New York: National Bureau of Economic Research, 1952).

[5] An exception is Werner Hirsch's time-series analysis of total spending for public education in the United States which is discussed below. A theoretical discussion of the determinants of government expenditures over time is contained in Alan T. Peacock and Jack Wiseman, *The Growth of Public Expenditures in the United Kingdom* (Princeton: National Bureau of Economic Research, 1961), 12-34.

[6] J. Frederic Dewhurst and Associates, *America's Needs and Resources* (New York: Twentieth Century Fund, 1955), 590-97.

concerned with planning for future public spending.[7] The procedure uses projections of population growth and its distribution by age and geographic location and forecasts of levels of national income and wealth to estimate the magnitudes of public needs and resources. Useful as such projections are, like the retrospective analysis of Dewhurst, they do not provide statistical estimates of the underlying determinants of governmental expenditures.

The absence of published statistical studies dealing with the determinants of total spending by all levels of government in the United States is matched by a similar paucity of systematic studies of the causes of changes over time in state and local expenditures. There is not a single widely known study of the relationship between historical changes in statewide economic and population characteristics and changes in the level of spending by a particular state. Fabricant discusses reasons for the growth in state and local expenditures.[8] There are studies that point to changes in population trends, industrialization, and other elements that have probably accounted for increased public spending in specific states.[9] But in these investigations systematic procedures for estimating the importance and relative magnitude of various factors considered are rarely used.

A major explanation for the lack of detailed time-series studies of public expenditures is the lack of yearly data for explanatory factors other than income and population. Also important is the difficulty of treating in a statistical time-series study the effects of changes in attitudes toward governmental responsibility for providing public services and the effects on public spending of international developments. The inability to apply time-series techniques to local government expenditures is a consequence not only of changing preferences and the lack of yearly estimates of crucial data but is also due to the changing boundaries of cities and special districts which make it

[7] Gerhard Colm and Manuel Helzner, "Financial Needs and Resources Over the Next Decade: At All Levels of Government," and Dick Netzer, "Financial Needs and Resources Over the Next Decade: State and Local Governments," in *Public Finances: Needs, Sources, and Utilization* (Princeton: National Bureau of Economic Research, 1961). See also Otto Eckstein, *Trends in Public Expenditures in the Next Decade* (Washington: Committee for Economic Development, 1959) and Robert Lampman, "How Much Government Spending in the 1960's?" I *The Quarterly Review of Economics and Business* (February 1961), 7-17.

[8] Fabricant, *op. cit.*, 134.

[9] For example, see Donald Davenport, *Report of Commission of Housing and Regional Planning* (Albany: J. B. Lyon Company, 1926).

impossible to obtain a set of observations for the same unit for a sufficient number of years.

In summarizing the circumstances that have led to the increase in public spending during the first six decades of the twentieth century it is necessary to rely on impressions derived from examinations of statistical series. There is no definitive analytic study that integrates these series and yields statistical estimates of the relative importance of various elements. The impressionistic studies attribute most of the long-term rise in total public expenditures in the United States to population growth, rising prices and incomes, increasing urbanization and industrialization, participation in two wars, and mounting peacetime military needs. Implicit in this list are several points worthy of separate mention. One is the recognition at all levels of government that in an industrial society unemployment, old age, and other forms of economic hardship must be ameliorated by public action including government spending. Another is the influence of changing technology and consumer tastes, and the effects of greater interdependence arising from urbanization and industrialization. All of these require increased public spending for highways, protection, public parks and recreation, enlarged educational programs, and information to businessmen, farmers, consumers, and other groups.

Changes in the social and economic structure have different influences on public spending at different levels of government. Rising prices have affected all levels of government. Wars and spending associated with foreign policy have led to considerable growth in federal spending. Also federal expenditures have been influenced by desires for economic stabilization and income redistribution, and to a lesser extent by federal participation in state and local programs for coping with public needs stemming from population growth and increased urbanization and industrialization. The states have had to deal directly with the demands for greater public services that arise when family incomes rise, the urban portion of the population grows, and industrialization occurs. Much of the responsibility for public spending necessitated by these developments has been delegated to local governments whose expenditures have, therefore, grown apace with state outlays.[10]

[10] An excellent brief discussion of these developments which contains much of the relevant data is in Arnold M. Soloway, "Growth of Government Over the Past 50 Years: An Analytical Review," in *Federal Expenditures Policy for Economic Growth and Stability* (Washington: Joint Economic Committee, 1957), 19-59.

Variations in Expenditures Among Governments

Analysis of the behavior of cities and states has dominated research on the determinants of variations in spending in a given year by similar kinds of governmental units. Despite data problems, counties, municipalities, and schools and other special districts are receiving more attention. The conventional procedure, in these cross-section studies, is to relate a series of independent variables, usually economic and demographic characteristics of the government under analysis, to its per capita public expenditures. Originally only simple correlations were computed but in recent work a multivariate statistical technique, often multiple regression, is used to estimate the net influence of each independent variable while other factors are taken into account. Often the study includes separate analyses of expenditures for such specific functions as police and fire protection, highways, education, and public welfare.

Differences in Expenditures Among States. Investigators of variations in public expenditures among states have treated the state as an integrated unit, combining state and local expenditures and studying this aggregate. This treatment avoids the problems arising out of the different patterns of state-local responsibility for government functions found among states. The effects of density, degree of urbanization, and state income on over-all state spending have received most attention. Contemporary students of state spending are devoting increased attention to the influence of state aid and alternative patterns of state and local government relations, and to discovering other economic and demographic differences among states associated with variations in public spending.

A seminar conducted by Gerhard Colm, using data from the 1932 Census of Governments, investigated the influence of density, urbanization, industrialization, and per capita income on state per capita total expenditures and on outlays for education, highways, and relief.[11] This study takes each variable into account singly and uses graphs which are evaluated by inspection. The 1942 Census of Governments, despite the abnormality of the war year, provided data for further studies of the determinants of state expenditures. Joseph Berolzheimer related population density and per capita income to measures of per capita state expenditures in 1942, using rank order classifications to illustrate relationships.[12] Fabricant, using data from

11 Gerhard Colm *et al.*, "Public Expenditures and Economic Structure in the United States," III *Social Research* (February 1936), 57-77.

12 Berolzheimer, *op. cit.* (March, April, May 1947), 170-77, 213-19, 237-44.

the same census, estimated by multiple regression the relationship of per capita income, degree of urbanization, and density to total expenditures per capita and to per capita spending for ten functional categories.[13] Fisher replicated Fabricant's approach for data from the 1957 Census of Governments.[14]

According to these studies, per capita income is the most important and most consistent determinant of state per capita expenditures. The influence of income is greatest in explaining total general expenditures by states and it has an especially close relationship to expenditures for highways and schools. As expected, income is relatively less important in outlays for basic local functions such as fire protection, sanitation, and public welfare.

Density, measured in population per square mile, is associated with slightly lower per capita expenditures for most functions. The negative influence of density occurs, according to Fabricant, "presumably because when public facilities can be used more intensively the cost of meeting specified levels of public service per head is lessened."[15] Higher density may, however, create conditions requiring increased public outlays to provide higher levels of police and health services.

Fabricant finds that the degree of urbanization, unlike density, does not have a significant effect on state expenditures. He and Fisher find that the greater the proportion of the population of a state living in urban places the greater are all general per capita expenditures as well as per capita outlays for public welfare, public safety, and sanitation. Both find spending for highways negatively related to urbanization.

The results of Colm's early, less rigorous study and Berolzheimer's rank order approach are substantially in agreement with the findings of Fabricant for 1942 and Fisher for 1957 in specifying which of the variables influence spending for various state functions. However, the ability of density, urbanization, and per capita income to predict state per capita expenditures has decreased since 1942. In that year the three variables explained about 72 per cent of the variance of total spending among states, while in 1957 the same variables accounted for 53 per cent. Similar reductions in the proportion of variance ex-

[13] Fabricant, *op. cit.*, 112-39.

[14] Glenn W. Fisher, "Determinants of State and Local Government Expenditures: A Preliminary Analysis," XIV *National Tax Journal* (December 1961), 349-55.

[15] Fabricant, *op. cit.*, 129.

plained in 1957 compared with 1942 prevail in other functional categories. Perhaps the secular growth in per capita income has provided opportunities for greater discretion and hence greater variability in state spending. In the earlier period low incomes may have limited public spending to the provision of basic public needs only—needs determined largely by density and urbanization. Further, levels of state spending in recent years have been far more strongly influenced by state aid programs which support outlays for highways, welfare, and education. None of these is closely related to urbanization or density.

The pioneer studies of state expenditures provided a point of reference for subsequent research and data collection and developed the beginnings of a methodology for analytic examination of public spending. Still, there are serious drawbacks to the use of independent variables such as urbanization and density which are gross measures that imperfectly encompass the underlying characteristics of an area. Further, it is doubtful that the same variables are appropriate for estimating expenditures for functions as diverse as welfare and education. There are currently several studies of state expenditures in progress that promise, through the use of computers and the full range of data now available, the investigation of a far more complete set of independent variables.

Differences in Expenditures Among Local Governments. Until recently the importance of understanding the determinants of local government expenditures was not reflected by the extent of analytic study of this subject. The problems of assembling a set of data showing expenditures and possible explanatory characteristics for a large number of local governments performing comparable functions were virtually insuperable. Simple studies relating population size and density to expenditures by cities and counties were all that could be done. Increased data collection by federal and state governments have now made possible greatly widened research in this area. Among the potential explanations of differences in levels of spending by local governments that have been studied are variations in income and wealth, population size and density, degree of urbanization and industrialization, state aid payments, and level and extent of public services provided.

Brazer's study of city expenditures is a highpoint in a gradually burgeoning series of statistical analyses of municipal expenditures.[16]

---

[16] Harvey E. Brazer, *City Expenditures in the United States* (New York: National Bureau of Economic Research, 1959).

Using multiple regression Brazer investigated for 1950 the determinants of total per capita general expenditures and of outlays for five major common functions in 462 large cities located throughout the United States. In addition, he examined separately cross-sections of cities in Ohio, Massachusetts, and California, and, finally, analyzed the expenditures of the 40 largest cities in the United States. Scott and Feder used multivariate techniques to study 40 California cities in 1950,[17] and Vieg and his associates considered 303 cities in California in a multiple-regression analysis.[18] Studies of municipal expenditures within metropolitan areas include Sacks and Hellmuth's study of 20 cities and 38 villages in metropolitan Cleveland,[19] Wood's factor analysis of 64 municipalities in the New York metropolitan area,[20] and an investigation of the 19 cities and villages of Milwaukee County by Schmandt and Stevens.[21]

Analytic studies of expenditures of counties and special districts are less frequent than those of cities. Vieg et al. examined the determinants of differences in county spending in California in 1956.[22] Hirsch investigated the relationship of expenditures and population size in 149 local governmental units in St. Louis County.[23]

Brazer's is the only study that analyzes determinants of expenditures by local governmental units located in different states. His findings for 462 cities of over 25,000 population emphasize family income, density, and intergovernmental revenues as crucial in determining per capita total general operating expenditures and virtually all specific municipal functions as well. A higher rate of growth of population lowers general operating expenditures and outlays for fire protection. Absolute population size is significant only in its positive effect on per capita spending for police protection. The proportion of population employed in manufacturing, trade, and services is positively associated

[17] Stanley Scott and Edward L. Feder, *Factors Associated with Variations in Municipal Expenditure Levels* (Berkeley: Bureau of Public Administration, University of California, 1957).

[18] John A. Vieg et al., *California Local Finance* (Stanford: Stanford University Press, 1960), 86-134.

[19] Seymour Sacks and William F. Hellmuth, Jr., *Financing Government in a Metropolitan Area* (New York: The Free Press of Glencoe, 1960), 68-153.

[20] Robert C. Wood, *1400 Governments* (Cambridge: Harvard University Press, 1961), 29-64, 217-34.

[21] Henry J. Schmandt and G. Ross Stephens, "Measuring Municipal Output," XIII *National Tax Journal* (December 1960), 369-75.

[22] Vieg et al., *op. cit.*

[23] Werner Z. Hirsch, "Expenditure Implications of Metropolitan Growth and Consolidation," XLI *Review of Economics and Statistics* (August 1959), 232-41.

with total expenditures for common functions and also with expenditures for police protection.

The three significant variables out of the six originally used in Brazer's regression explain 57 per cent of the variance in spending for total general operating expenditures among the 462 largest cities located throughout the United States. Brazer's equation, thus, is roughly as accurate in predicting over-all city expenditures in 1950 as is Fisher's equation in predicting over-all state expenditures in 1957. But density is negative in its impact on state spending and positive in its effect on city spending. The higher costs of police and fire protection and sanitation in the cities is offset in the state analysis by the negative influence of density on highway and school expenditures. Also income, so important in explaining state expenditures, is not significant in explaining total general operating expenditures of cities.

The results of Scott and Feder's study of cities in California and the portion of Brazer's study dealing with cities in that state are fundamentally similar wherever the same variables are used. Both find population size and population density insignificant and the rate of population increase significantly negative in its influence on per capita general expenditures. The measure of capacity to pay is most important in both analyses; Brazer used median family income and Scott and Feder per capita market value of property. The analysis of 303 cities in California by Vieg *et al.* shows per capita assessed value of property most important and finds population size also significant. Levels of property assessments, however, are often the consequence of expenditure decisions and not their determinants. That is, expenditure levels are set and then assessments adjusted in light of property tax rates to yield revenues equal to the already determined expenditures. In practice both tax rates and assessments can be changed in response to increased local budgets. Where assessments are more flexible than tax rates, assessed value of property is less an independent variable than a proxy for the dependent variable, and, of course, is highly correlated with it. This problem of treating as independent a variable whose value is in some way influenced by the size of the dependent variable arises also in Brazer's use of intergovernmental revenue as an independent variable.[24] Occasionally this difficulty cannot be avoided entirely, but results must be viewed with caution when it may be present.

Additional findings of these and other studies are fragmentary and conflicting. Hirsch, in an analysis of the relationship of population

---

[24] Brazer is aware of this problem and comments on it in *op. cit.*, 22-23.

size and expenditures for particular functions by governments located in St. Louis County, finds little evidence supporting the presence of economies of scale. He argues that consolidation into units serving larger numbers of people is not likely to reduce governmental costs. Schmandt and Stevens in their study of spending in Milwaukee County conclude to the contrary, that governmental units of larger size are likely to be more efficient in providing a given level of service, but that higher per capita expenditures are associated with larger population size because increased service levels are needed and provided in larger sized governmental units. The importance of variations in state-local government relationships is illustrated by Brazer's finding of different effects on expenditures of the same variable in cities in California, Ohio, and Massachusetts.

There is, in the conflicting and incomplete picture of the determinants of state and local government spending, clear evidence that all of the essential variables have not yet been sorted out; that a uniformly effective treatment of factors known to be important has not been discovered; and that the highly important effects of intergovernmental relations on local spending have not yet been adequately treated in the empirical models. Still, it is also clear that family income is a key determinant of most city expenditures, that the amount of intergovernmental revenue per capita is crucial, and that population density is quite important in explaining expenditures for police, sanitation, and highways. Furthermore, absolute population size is consistently found to be unrelated to expenditures, but if service level is taken into account there is tentative evidence of economies of scale in public spending for certain purposes.

STUDIES OF SPENDING FOR PUBLIC EDUCATION

Because expenditures for public education are the largest of any single state and local government function, almost all analyses of the determinants of public expenditures by economists, political scientists, and public administrators specifically discuss outlays for education. In addition, students of educational finance have investigated the forces that shape these expenditures. Analysis of the determinants of the historical growth in spending for local schools in the United States, for the most part, has dealt with the causes of variations in expenditures among states. Explanations of sources of variations in expenditures by school districts have seldom been attempted because school district boundaries frequently do not coincide with areas for which the Bureau of the Census collects data.

Growth in Outlays for Public Education

Since 1900 total outlays for local public education in the United States have risen from $238 million to over $15 billion. During this period, spending for local schools has grown from 25 to 35 per cent of total general state and local expenditures. There is general agreement among students of public school finance that price increases, growth in enrollments and in the proportion of high school students, higher levels of per capita personal income, improved educational services, and changing attitudes toward education all have had a part in the historical rise in spending for public schools. Presentation of statistics comparing rates of growth in these and other factors to the increase in educational spending is informative, but does not demonstrate the relative importance and systematic influence of the various elements. An analytic approach is necessary to accomplish this.

The most ambitious and extensive analytic examination of the growth of expenditures for public education in the United States that has been published[25] is a study by Werner Z. Hirsch.[26] In analyzing the rising costs of public education Hirsch suggests six categories of factors that affect expenditure level and tries to quantify them for the period 1900-1958. The categories are (1) number of pupils in average daily attendance, (2) sociological characteristics of the population (largely age and geographic distributions), (3) economic characteristics (prices and incomes), (4) variety, scope, and quality of educational services, (5) productivity of schools, and (6) government responsibility. Quantitative measures of the first four of these factors include average daily attendance, high school enrollment relative to total enrollment, length of school term, proportion of pupils from urban areas, average annual salaries of teachers, per capital national income, and the number of supervisory and auxiliary employees per 1,000 pupils. With one exception all of these measures rose steadily from 1900 to 1958 as did total and per pupil expenditures for public elementary and secondary education. Only the proportion of pupils from urban areas lags, probably because many of the suburbs into which people moved after World War II have not yet been classified as urban places.

25 An extensive state-by-state study of the determinants of historical and cross-sectional expenditures for elementary and secondary education has recently been completed by Sherman Shapiro of Notre Dame University as a doctoral dissertation for the University of Chicago. See below, in this chapter.

26 Werner Z. Hirsch, *Analysis of the Rising Costs of Public Education* (Washington: Joint Economic Committee, 1959).

The two remaining factors are less fully studied by Hirsch. Educational productivity cannot be measured directly because much of educational output is nonquantifiable. Hirsch concludes that while it is difficult to assess changes in productivity in public education, increased use of television, group teaching, and available plant may reduce the need for increased outlays by raising productivity. The locus of governmental responsibility for local schools is also important in influencing spending, according to Hirsch. However, because he is not studying spending by individual states, Hirsch does not explore the effects of various patterns of governmental responsibilities.

In an effort to draw together the effects of the elements that influence educational expenditures Hirsch performs two multiple regressions using time-series analysis for 1900-1958. The dependent variable is daily total current expenditures plus debt service for elementary and secondary education per pupil in average daily attendance. This form of the dependent variable takes into account the average number of pupils in daily attendance and the length of the school year. Among the independent variables are teachers' salaries, proportion of high school students, per cent of pupils living in urban areas, number of supervisory and auxiliary personnel per 1,000 pupils, and per capita income. Of these, only salary level and per capita income are found to be significant. Moreover, each of these variables has a simple correlation coefficient of over .97 with the dependent variable. Salary level and per capita income are so highly intercorrelated for the period studied that they are, in effect, statistically the same variable in different forms.

Hirsch uses the results of the regression in which per capita income is employed to estimate income elasticity of demand for education and finds it to be 1.09 for 1900-1958. Since income elasticity is the percentage change in expenditures associated with a 1 per cent change in income, Hirsch's finding implies that on the average during 1900-1958 for every 1 per cent rise in per capita national income an additional 1.09 per cent was spent per pupil per day for elementary and secondary public education.

A more comprehensive analysis of income elasticity of educational outlays over time is contained in a thesis by Eugene P. McLoone.[27] McLoone estimates state-by-state elasticities and an average for the United States for four different time periods: 1929-30 to 1957-58, 1929-30 to 1943-44, 1943-44 to 1957-58, and 1947-48 to 1957-58. Elasticity

[27] Eugene P. McLoone, *Effects of Tax Elasticity on the Financial Support of Education* (unpublished doctoral dissertation, University of Illinois, 1961).

is measured as the percentage change in current expenditures per pupil in average daily attendance associated with a 1 per cent change in per capita personal income, and is estimated on the basis of a simple regression of these two variables.

For the nation as a whole McLoone finds that over the period 1929-30 to 1957-58 the gross income elasticity of education was .99, a figure similar to that found by Hirsch for 1900-1958. Among individual states only four deviated from this national average by more than 20 per cent for this period. The nationwide elasticity varied from a low of .46 for 1929-30 to 1943-44 (when the depression and the press of wartime needs lessened the priority of educational spending) to a high of 1.61 during the postwar period from 1943-44 to 1957-58. The low priority of public education from 1929 to 1944 is reflected in the estimates of state-by-state elasticity, none of which exceed .74. On the other hand, as an indication of educational efforts since World War II, no state has an income elasticity below 1.0 for the period 1943-44 to 1957-58. In the most recent period, 1947-48 to 1957-58, income elasticities range around the national average of 1.34 with four states falling below 1.0 and three having income elasticities above 2.0.

McLoone's results indicate that the relatively low income elasticity found by Hirsch for 1900-1958 probably reflects the low elasticities of 1929-1944 as well as low elasticities during the earlier part of the century. Recent behavior of educational spending indicates a responsiveness to increases in per capita personal income of greater than unit elasticity.

A further investigation by Thomas James of the response of educational expenditures to changes in personal income in five states provides another statistical estimate of the effects of income on individual state spending for education over time.[28] James estimates by linear regression the relationship of total state personal income to total state expenditures for education during 1946-1958 separately for Washington, California, New Jersey, Wisconsin, and Nebraska. No other independent variables were included. James reports his results in terms of regression coefficients, but for comparison with the results of Hirsch and McLoone these coefficients can be converted to elasticities around the mean, and as such they vary from a high of 2.12 for Nebraska to a low of 1.49 for New Jersey. The relatively high elasticities reflect, partially, the inclusion of outlays for higher educa-

[28] H. Thomas James, *School Revenue Systems in Five States* (Stanford: School of Education, Stanford University, 1961), 72-76.

tion and capital construction in the figures for educational expenditures. Still, their magnitude is further evidence of a greater than proportionate responsiveness of educational spending to income increases in the postwar period.

Income elasticities in the studies discussed above are not directly comparable because of differences in the time span covered, the definition of expenditures for education, the number of independent variables included simultaneously with income, and the contrast between nationwide and state-by-state analyses.

Although increases in income have received most stress in explanations of rising expenditures for education in individual states, changes in other factors are also important. There is no single systematic study of changes in demographic, social, and governmental characteristics of states and their rising educational spending. Edward F. Renshaw has estimated the statewide response to increases in state aid per pupil by means of a difference equation in which differences in expenditures per pupil between 1945 and 1949 are related to differences in per capita income and differences in state aid per pupil during these years.[29] Renshaw finds that increased state aid payments systematically lead to higher expenditures per pupil. For every dollar of increase in state aid from 1945 to 1949, expenditures per pupil rose by about 40 cents. Rising per capita income during this period resulted on the average in only a seven-cent rise in spending. Changes in state aid and income explained less than 10 per cent of the variance of the difference in state expenditures between 1945 and 1949.

Renshaw suggests that short-run changes in per capita income are not necessarily interpreted as making the community permanently wealthier and so there is low responsiveness of educational outlays. Higher incomes must persist before they are perceived as being a permanent indication of a greater ability to support higher levels of school spending. It is possible, however, that the consequence of increases in state incomes is a rise in tax revenues and, therefore, a willingness to increase state aid payments. Thus, rising incomes still may determine increases in educational spending, but by the indirect route of higher state aid. On the other hand, Renshaw's results may be interpreted as indicating that simple income elasticities such as McLoone's overestimate the net effect of income because they do not take into account the influence of other factors that have increased along with income, such as rising state aid payments.

    [29] Edward F. Renshaw, "A Note on the Expenditure Effect of Aid to Education," LXVII *Journal of Political Economy* (April 1960), 170-74.

There are a few fragments of research on the determinants of changes in expenditures in individual school systems over time. A study by Lohnes sought to determine whether the percentage change in total current expenditures from 1950 to 1955 in the 350 school systems in Massachusetts, Boston excepted, was related in a systematic way to the rate of growth in enrollments and the absolute size of the school system.[30] Analysis of variance applied to the data indicates that differences in the rate of growth in enrollments are directly associated with higher percentage increases in expenditures. School system size also is related to rate of change in expenditures; medium sized school systems (500 to 1,999 pupils) had greater relative increases in spending than small (0-499) or large (2,000 to 28,000) systems when differences in rate of growth of enrollments is held constant.

Another brief investigation of changes in individual school system expenditures over time is contained in the Sacks-Hellmuth study of metropolitan Cleveland.[31] Using the 32 school systems in the metropolitan area the authors studied changes in total operating expenditures for 1950-1958. The three independent variables employed were changes in assessed valuation, changes in average daily membership, and changes in state aid. Individually each of these independent variables is found to be highly correlated with changes in educational spending by individual school districts between 1950 and 1958. A multivariate analysis, taking all three into account simultaneously, reveals that changes in assessed valuation are far more important than changes in numbers of pupils or amounts of state aid in accounting for increases in spending over time by a local school district. As has been said before, if tax rates remain unchanged, changes in assessed valuation may be the result of a decision to spend more and not the determinant of such a decision. These results would be more significant if a measure of equalized or market value of property had been available and had been used instead.

While there are no other major statistical studies of the historical growth of total expenditures for elementary and secondary public education in the United States, almost all projections of future governmental expenditures based on extrapolations of past trends include a separate educational component. These projections are nationwide in scope, take account of the growth in total enrollments and in the

[30] Paul R. Lohnes, *New England Finances Public Education* (Cambridge: New England School Development Council, 1958).
[31] Sacks and Hellmuth, *op. cit.*, 107-08.

proportion of high school students, and make some allowance for improved educational services. Price increases usually are ignored because the projections are intended to show relative growth in expenditure needs and the resources for providing them, and it is presumed that price increases leave relative public needs and resources unchanged.[32]

Results of these studies of the growth of public spending for education only partially support the impressions of less analytic observers. All the studies confirm that rising per capita incomes have contributed to the growth in educational spending, although estimates of the importance of income vary depending on the particular measure of spending studied and on the other factors considered simultaneously with income. Increases in the amounts of state aid payments over time appear highly related to rising educational outlays, and when considered with income reduce the net influence of income. But the cause and effect relationship between rising state aid payments and increasing state incomes is not clear. Rising expenditures are associated with increases in assessed valuation of property, but, here again, not knowing the direction of the relationship between changes in expenditures and changes in property assessments renders this finding inconclusive. Rapid growth in enrollment and the size of the school system are associated with higher percentage increases in spending. Other variables such as the rising proportion of high school enrollment and the growth in administrative and other nonteaching personnel have not been verified, statistically, as contributing to rising educational spending.

There is little in these results that is absolutely contradictory, yet the piecemeal consideration of independent variables is not conducive to definitive conclusions. Fruitful research in this area requires multivariate study of changes in other factors considered jointly with changes in levels of income.

Variations in Outlays for Public Education Among States

In any year there is a wide variation in spending for education among states. Differences are found whether state spending is measured on a per pupil or per capita basis or as a portion of state income. Per capita income, density, and degree of urbanization, the variables most frequently used to explain differences in total spending by state

[32] See, for example, Netzer, op. cit., and Eckstein, op. cit., and Paying for Better Public Schools (New York: Committee for Economic Development, 1959), 13-30.

governments, are also applied to explaining variations in educational outlays by states. In addition, certain other factors believed especially germane to education have been investigated. They include both the amount and the proportion of local school revenues from state and federal sources, the proportion of school age children in the population, the proportion of children not attending public schools, the amount of property valuation in the state, and the proportion of non-whites in the population.

Many studies that explore the determinants of differences in overall expenditures among states also include education as one of the fundamental categories of spending to be investigated. Colm[33] for 1932, Berholzheimer[34] and Fabricant[35] for 1942, and Fisher[36] for 1957 relate statewide per capita expenditures for local education to per capita income, density, and degree of urbanization. Fisher and Fabricant, using multiple-regression analysis, and Colm and Berolzheimer, using less technical methods, are in agreement that higher densities and per capita incomes are associated with higher per capita outlays for public education. The influence of urbanization on educational spending is negative in Fabricant's study for 1942 and positive in Fisher's for 1957, but its negative effect is not significant in Fabricant's study while Fisher does not present the standard errors necessary to determine significance. The three variables, density, urbanization, and per capita income, explain 63 per cent of the variance in local school spending among the states in 1957 and 58 per cent of all school spending, including state colleges and universities, among states in 1942.

In a cross-section study devoted only to expenditures for education Walter McMahon examined the determinants of state educational spending as a proportion of state disposable income for 1956.[37] The measure of state effort was related to such statewide characteristics as proportion of school-age children in the population, number of children not in public schools as a percentage of those in average daily attendance, proportion of non-whites, population density, disposable income of the previous year, and state and federal aid as a per cent of total expenditures on education. Although most of these independent variables had significant simple correlations with the

[33] Colm, *op. cit.*
[34] Berolzheimer, *op. cit.*
[35] Fabricant, *op. cit.*, 122-31.
[36] Fisher, *op. cit.*
[37] Walter W. McMahon, "The Determinants of Public Expenditure: An Econometric Analysis of the Demand for Public Education" (unpublished paper, Urbana: Department of Economics, University of Illinois).

ratio of expenditures to income, only three, the proportion of children in the population, the proportion of non-whites, and the proportion of children not attending public schools, were significant in the multivariate analysis, accounting for 52 per cent of the variance. McMahon interprets the results as showing that relative state effort for education depends on the need for educational services measured by the proportion of youngsters in the population. In addition, effort is inversely related to the use of nonpublic schools and to early dropout as well as to the disenfranchisement of certain groups of the population with substantial needs for education but few means. This phenomenon is reflected by the effect of the proportion of non-whites in the population. Educational effort among states, measured as the ratio of expenditures to income, appears to be unrelated to the absolute level of state disposable income, the relative importance of state and federal aid, and population density.

An analysis by Edward F. Renshaw indicates that although the ratio of state aid to expenditures is not related to educational effort, the amount of state aid per pupil is related to expenditures per pupil.[38] Renshaw, in a study of state spending per pupil in 1949-50, finds that state aid per pupil is virtually significant at the .95 level in a multiple regression in which the other independent variables, per capita state income and percentage of non-white population, are both more systematic in their effects on spending than state aid. Together they explain 65 per cent of the variance in state spending in 1949-50.

According to Renshaw's estimates, on the average a dollar of state aid leads to 16 cents of educational spending while a dollar of per capita income gives rise to 14 cents of educational expenditures per pupil. From these figures Renshaw concludes that about 84 per cent of state aid is a substitute for local support. Many state aid programs are designed precisely to substitute for local support, and Renshaw's conclusions would be disheartening only if state aid were intended to be a stimulant of local support. However, he writes that additional examination of residuals from the equation "fails to reveal any evidence that would strongly support one method of granting state aid as being superior to other methods in terms of the resulting expenditure effect." It does appear, then, that incentive-based aid programs are no more successful in generating local support than equalization programs.

The most comprehensive study of educational expenditures among

[38] Renshaw, *op. cit.*

states has been conducted by Sherman Shapiro.[39] This work consists of a series of cross-section analyses for 1920, 1930, 1940, and 1950, of state-by-state expenditures for education. There are two dependent variables; one is a measure of current public expenditures per pupil for elementary and secondary education and the other adds corresponding private educational outlays to get what Shapiro calls societal expenditures. In addition to an analysis of all states for each of the four decade years, there are separate analyses of the South and the non-South. The method used not only permits the investigation of the effects of independent variables in a given year and of relationships for major regions of the United States, but also allows periodic comparison of changes in these effects over a span of four decades.

Shapiro suggests that two broad hypotheses are tested by his analysis: "1. Certain socio-economic factors operate to determine levels of expenditure regardless of region. 2. The relative importance of the explanatory factors will not be the same [between regions and among years]." Altogether eleven socio-economic independent variables were examined at different stages of the analysis, but at no time were more than seven included in the same regression. In an exploratory phase four socio-economic variables were investigated and discarded. Percentage non-white was eliminated because the racial variable had no important explanatory power within regions, although it was important in the analysis of the United States as a whole. Shapiro decided to use a general regional variable to account for this and other effects attributable to factors unimportant within regions, but important because of their contribution to the study of all states; they indicate what he terms "regional trait complexes." Relative enrollment in private schools generally was not significant in the exploratory analysis nor was the percentage of population aged 5 to 17. The extent of urbanization, while significant in the regressions for 1920, is replaced in the final analysis by a measure of industrialization which yields a more regular pattern of relationships.

In the final phase there are six regressions for each year; three have public expenditures as the dependent variable, and three societal expenditures. Each of the two dependent variables is analyzed for the United States as a whole and for the South and non-South separately. Per capita personal income by state and the percentage of the

[39] Sherman Shapiro, unpublished doctoral dissertation, University of Chicago, 1962. Major results of the study have been published: Sherman Shapiro, "Some Socioeconomic Determinants of Expenditures for Education: Southern and Other States Compared," 6 *Comparative Education Review* (October 1962), 160-66.

civilian labor force in nonagricultural employment are included as independent variables in regressions for both public and societal expenditures. The regressions on public expenditures also include the percentage of children aged 5 to 17 enrolled in public schools and the percentage of total enrollment in public high schools. These latter two variables are replaced, in the analysis of societal expenditures, by the percentage of children and of high school pupils enrolled in private as well as public schools. Thus, each of the dependent variables is related to a set of four similar but not identical independent factors. A fifth variable, the regional "dummy variable" which takes account of systematic variations among regions, is added for analyses of the United States as a whole.

The set of four independent variables explains for the nation as a whole about 45 to 70 per cent of the variance of educational expenditures, and when the regional "dummy variable" is added, the proportion of variance explained rises to from two-thirds to almost nine-tenths. In the analysis by regions the regression equations explain from half to over four-fifths of the variance in educational spending among southern states and two-fifths to two-thirds of the variance for the other states. The contribution of the regional variable to the explanation of interstate variations in educational expenditures declines in importance between 1920 and 1940, although there is no indication of a further decline in 1950. Shapiro concludes that regional differences have dropped sharply over the period from 1920 to 1950, but this seems a bit of an overstatement since the wartime years between 1940 and 1950 are generally believed to have been a period of great regional homogenization. By Shapiro's reasoning this should have produced a further reduction in the importance of the regional variable in the regression for 1950.

In the over-all multivariate regressions state per capita personal income contributes most to the explanation of both public and societal per pupil educational expenditures in all years except 1920. Simple correlations between state income and educational expenditures are all positive and are higher for the South than for the non-South. The regional multivariate analyses indicate, however, that when other determinants of educational spending are taken into account, income has had a significantly positive effect on expenditures in the non-South, but, generally, no significant effect in the South.

School attendance rates are a significant positive factor in most of the non-South regressions for both private and societal expenditures. The proportion in secondary schools, however, does not show any regular relationship with per pupil expenditures in the four years studied. Degree of industrialization, measured by nonagricultural employment, is significant only in a single regression, but in all years studied the direction of its effect is negative for the non-South and positive for the South.

The recent study by Thomas James had as one of its primary hypotheses that increased state support of local school spending reduces variations in outlays among school systems within a state.[40] This study falls between a consideration of statewide expenditures and those of individual school districts. James sampled a total of 316 school systems of over 1,500 pupils each in the states of Washington, California, New Jersey, Nebraska, and Wisconsin. For each of these states James computed the coefficient of variation of per pupil spending for the school system in his sample. These coefficients of variation were then related to the amount of state-provided revenue per pupil. With the exception of Nebraska, James finds that the variation in per pupil spending falls as state aid per pupil rises. He concludes that his hypothesis is not refuted and plans to seek further evidence in a second phase, as yet uncompleted, of his study.

Although James is primarily interested in the variability of spending by school systems in different states, he also explores some concomitant variables affecting expenditures for education. He notes that for the four states other than California neither the amount of taxable valuation per pupil nor the amount of state aid per pupil correlates highly with expenditures per pupil. In four states the correlation of state aid expenditures is negative. These simple correlations further demonstrate that factors other than taxable valuation and state aid must be considered simultaneously if the true net effect of these variables is to be revealed.

Private school enrollment as a per cent of total school-age population is not related to the level of per pupil expenditures in the states studied by James. In contrast to this finding, McMahon found for all states a simple correlation of −.33 between expenditure effort and the broader measure of the proportion of children not in public schools. Furthermore, this variable was significant in McMahon's multiple regression. Tentative examination of the relative effects of independent and dependent school district organization for New Jersey and Wisconsin leads James to conclude that "wealth factors, per capita income, per household income, and property valuations

40 James, *op. cit.*, 29-71.

tend to influence expenditures more in fiscally independent districts than in the dependent ones." Finally, James briefly examines the relationship of the type of community in which a school system is located and its per pupil expenditure. He finds that for all five states taken together the highest expenditures per pupil are made in industrial suburbs and the lowest in independent cities that have no functional connection with a larger metropolis. If property values per pupil are taken into account the major metropolitan core cities and the industrial suburbs spend more relative to their property tax base than do resort cities, residential suburbs and other cities located outside of the major metropolitan core areas.

Variations of Outlays for Public Education Among School Systems

Empirical studies relating expenditures to economic, social, demographic, and other characteristics of individual school systems have been seriously hindered by the generally noncoterminous boundaries of school districts and other governmental units. Still, the importance of analyzing the individual school system, which is after all the basic decision-making unit in determining spending for local schools, has led to several efforts to collect and study detailed data for such units.

An early discussion of the factors in a community that might influence the characteristics of individual schools is Mort and Cornell's *Adaptability of Public School Systems* published in 1938.[41] This book acted as a statement of hypotheses which were tested first by the authors in a study of 36 Pennsylvania communities and later by a host of students at Teachers College at Columbia University. The formation in 1942 of the Metropolitan School Study Council, consisting of 28 school systems in the New York metropolitan area, provided a further testing ground for new formulations of the original hypotheses. By 1956 the number of school systems in the Council had expanded to 83 and much data had been collected and analyzed.[42]

The major purpose of the Metropolitan School Study Council and the Pennsylvania study was to determine, quantitatively, the extent to which different community characteristics were associated with the adoption of educational practices deemed desirable by Mort, Cornell, and other educational experts. In addition to measuring the complex

[41] Paul R. Mort and Francis G. Cornell, *Adaptability of Public School Systems* (New York: Teachers College, Columbia University, 1938).

[42] A detailed description of research on adaptability of local schools is found in Donald H. Ross, ed., *Administration for Adaptability* (New York: Metropolitan School Study Council, 1958).

relationships among factors associated with measures of adaptability the researchers computed simple correlations between current expenditures per pupil and the community and school system characteristics they were investigating.

As expected, internal school characteristics and per pupil expenditures were found to be highly correlated. Larger expenditures occur in school systems that employ more highly trained and experienced staffs. Turning to community characteristics and spending, analysis of the Metropolitan School Study Council data for 28 school systems shows that wealth of a school district, the time trend of the growth of this wealth, and tax leeway (related to wealth) are the factors most highly correlated with school spending. The importance of wealth is further illustrated by the negative correlation of over .50 for two measures of tax rates; high tax rates imply less school spending per pupil but are necessary to provide educational services in communities with low property valuations. No nonfinancial characteristics were found that were strongly associated with school spending. The proportion of population over 50 years of age and the proportion owning their own homes both are correlated about .30 with expenditures, but these two factors may be proxies for family income and the correlations may be spurious. The number of pupils enrolled and the proportion of unskilled workers in the community tend to be associated with lower outlays for education, although the correlations are only .16. Other characteristics such as density, area, proportion of college graduates and of business and professional workers were not found to be systematically related to levels of expenditures per pupil.

The findings of the Metropolitan School Study Council with regard to the determinants of local school expenditures must be interpreted with restraint. The intent of the Council and those who have gathered and analyzed the data was primarily to study adaptability and not expenditures. Simple correlations with expenditures do not necessarily reveal the presence or absence of net relationships that would emerge from multiple correlation. Further, the limited number and geographical scope of the school systems studied restrict the generality of the conclusions. Nonetheless, these findings were for many years the only information in this area, and remain among the vital sources for preliminary examination in developing new hypotheses regarding the relationships between the nature of the community and the financial support of local schools.

A more direct multivariate study of the determinants of educational spending in individual school systems is an analysis of 26 school districts in St. Louis County by Werner Hirsch.[43] Hirsch employs the same framework that he used in his study of the growth in educational spending to guide the selection of quantitative measures of factors that influence spending in local school systems. The basic dependent variable is total current expenditures plus debt service for elementary and secondary education per pupil in average daily attendance. In addition, per pupil expenditures for general control, instruction, auxiliary services, plant operation and maintenance, and fixed charges all are analyzed as separate dependent variables. The independent variables include number of pupils in average daily attendance, number of public schools per square mile, per cent increase in average daily attendance 1951-1956, an index of scope and quality of education, and assessed valuation per pupil. Hirsch omits any independent variable for state aid to local schools because, during the period studied, the state provided virtually nothing under its equalization program.

Unfortunately, the reliability of Hirsch's results are somewhat equivocal because he used data for two different periods from the same districts as a way of increasing the number of observations and hence the degrees of freedom. The relationships between dependent and independent variables for the same school district at a two-year interval are likely to be far more similar than relationships for different school districts in the same year. If so, the actual degrees of freedom are fewer than the number used by Hirsch and, therefore, the correlations are overestimated.

Assessed valuation, scope and quality of education, and per cent of high school pupils in average daily attendance are statistically significant in the regression on current expenditures; all six independent variables explain about 82 per cent of the total variance. Assessed valuation and the scope and quality of education may not be determinants of expenditures but may instead be determined by decisions regarding the level of expenditures. If so, the large portion of variance accounted for by them in Hirsch's regression equations is not exclusively an indication of their influence on school spending but may be partly the statistical consequence of treating a component of the dependent variable as an independent variable.

The number of pupils in average daily attendance is not significant in the regression, and Hirsch finds no evidence of economies of scale in local education.[44] Neither the number of schools per square

[43] Werner Z. Hirsch, "Determinants of Public Education Expenditures," XIII National Tax Journal (March 1960), 29-40.

[44] Schmandt and Stephens, op. cit., 375, write that their study "strongly

mile, a measure of density, nor percentage increase in enrollment are significant. The density measure has the expected negative sign, but larger percentage increases in enrollment appear, unexpectedly, to be associated with lower expenditures. Perhaps the press of other public and private needs in growing communities results in a less than proportionate flow of resources to education, or possibly response lags are not adequately taken into account in Hirsch's formulation.

The absence of a measure of per capita or family income leads Hirsch to use assessed property valuation as a proxy for income in an analysis of the income elasticity of various components of educational spending. Despite the imperfections of this proxy, the results are most revealing. The income elasticities (assessed property value elasticities) are estimated at the mean and are determined from a multiple regression that includes all but one of the independent variables mentioned in the previous paragraph. Scope and quality of education is omitted because Hirsch regards it as a consequence rather than a determinant of income elasticity. According to this equation the effects of a one per cent change in the amount of assessed property valuation (interpreted as a change in income) is a greater than one per cent increase only in expenditures for auxiliary services. Total current expenditures, expenditures for plant operation and maintenance, and general control expenditures increase by about one half of one per cent in response to a one per cent rise in income. Outlays for instruction have an elasticity of .42, the least responsive of all categories of expenditure except fixed charges.

A more simple approach to explaining variations in expenditures among individual school systems is used by Sacks and Hellmuth in their wide ranging study of governmental finances in metropolitan Cleveland.[45] For the 32 school districts in the area Sacks and Hellmuth analyze total school operating expenditures and per pupil operating expenditures in 1956. The independent variables chosen were number of pupils in average daily membership, the amount of assessed property valuation, and the amount of state aid; for the analysis of per pupil expenditures a fourth independent variable, the amount of personal wealth per pupil, was included. Differences in the number of students and in state aid account for virtually all of the variance in total school spending. The effect of differences in the amount of assessed property valuation is trivial when the other two variables

suggests the existence of economies of scale in school district operations in the Milwaukee area" when a measure of service output is used in conjunction with average daily attendance.

[45] Sacks and Hellmuth, *op. cit.*, 100-01.

are also taken into account. The results of the analysis of per pupil expenditures are strongly influenced by the introduction of personal wealth which contributes heavily to the portion of variance explained. State aid is considerably less important in accounting for differences in per pupil spending among school districts than in total spending. Assessed valuation and the number of pupils are found to be unimportant.

The considerable importance of assessed valuation in explaining per pupil spending among school districts in St. Louis County is not duplicated in the analysis of school districts in metropolitan Cleveland. Introducing personal wealth into the equation for the Cleveland area provides what appears to be a more direct factor reflecting capacity to support education than the amount of assessed valuation.

Brazer's study of city expenditures emphasizes functions that are common to all cities and, consequently, educational spending received only limited attention. Many cities do not operate the school systems that provide education to their residents and spending for schools is not included in their budgets. However, Brazer obtained data on educational spending for his analysis of the forty largest cities in the United States.[46] While this coverage is far from representative, it is the only statistical study that combines, in a single analysis, spending for education by governments located in different states. Furthermore, Brazer's dependent variable is in per capita terms, a measure of more interest to economists and political scientists than the per pupil expenditure figures that educators stress.

Brazer's findings reveal median family income as the most important factor in explaining difference in per capita educational spending among cities. Not surprisingly, the need for school services measured by the number of students in average daily attendance per 1,000 population is also important as is the amount of intergovernmental revenue per pupil. A high proportion of city residents to the population of the entire metropolitan area is a negative influence on educational spending in large cities. Brazer's general interpretation of higher city spending when the suburban area is relatively large is the cost of public services provided by cities to suburban residents who work and shop in the central city. This explanation, although applicable to other expenditure categories, does not seem applicable to educational spending since city schools do not provide services to suburbanites. Density and the amount of employment in manufacturing and trade, the other independent variables used by Brazer, are not significant determinants of educational expenditures in these cities.

46 Brazer, op. cit., 59-60.

Elasticities for the variables in city spending for education emphasize the importance of family income. A 1 per cent rise in median family income is associated with a rise of about .7 per cent in spending. For intergovernmental revenue per pupil, the relative number of students in the population, and the ratio of city population to total metropolitan population, the elasticity coefficients did not exceed .27.

COMPARISON OF STUDIES

The income elasticity of spending for education of .7 found by Brazer for 40 large cities in 1950 is quite close to the elasticity of .8 computed by Fabricant for states in 1942 and both are higher than the coefficient of .5 estimated in Hirsch's study of school districts in St. Louis County. Direct comparison of these elasticities is inappropriate not only because three different measures of income are used but also because Brazer and Fabricant treat expenditures on a per capita basis and Hirsch on a per pupil basis. Both Renshaw and Brazer estimate the effect of state aid on educational spending. According to Brazer the average net effect of a one-dollar increase in state aid per pupil in large cities is to increase per capita spending on education by 29 cents. Renshaw, analyzing the 48 continental states, estimates the net effect on per pupil school spending of a one-dollar increase in state aid at 16 cents. The difference in the measure of school spending restricts the implications that can be drawn from comparisons, although one would expect the influence of state aid to be greater on per pupil than on per capita spending.

These studies attribute most of the explained variation in spending for local public schools to differences in income, property valuation, state aid payments, the number of pupils in relation to population, and the proportion of pupils in secondary grades. The importance of these factors varies from study to study. It is possible that the variations in the effects of similar independent variables in studies for different areas reflect actual differences in response. But, differences in the character of the dependent variable, the number and nature of the independent variables used, and other variations in study design make it impossible to synthesize the results of existing research. Further, data problems have limited the introduction into these studies of demographic and social factors such as education and occupation of parents. The study undertaken here incorporates population characteristics into the analysis and, within the same study design, examines the behavior of a wide sampling of school systems in different areas. Thus, the study seeks to remedy several major shortcomings in the pattern of existing studies of determinants of local school spending.

IV. Formulation of an Empirical Model

THE CHARACTERISTICS of the empirical study are described in this chapter. First, a contrast is drawn between economic and political approaches to the explanation of government behavior, and the general approach used in this study is described briefly. Next, the reasoning underlying the selection of the specific dependent and independent variables is set forth. The final sections contain a discussion of the sample, the data, and the method of analysis.

ALTERNATIVE APPROACHES

Two broadly different approaches to government behavior have been built on the foundation of a focus on the public decision-making body. The political approach treats the attainment of political support by incumbent officeholders as the fundamental objective. Governmental spending, in this view, is either the direct result of voter preferences expressed in referenda or, more often, the consequence of decisions made by elected or appointed officials who endeavor to remain in office by providing those public services which they believe the electorate desires. Anthony Downs has formulated the essentials of a theory that describes how governments would react to different circumstances under the assumption "that every government seeks to maximize political support."[1] On this assumption Downs derives a complex set of principles of decision-making such that, given the preferences of the electorate, political leaders maximize their chances for reelection. This approach is extremely general and can be applied to all areas of government action.[2] In this framework the primary task of the politician is to advocate a uniform policy for all citizens which will garner the most votes, and consensus is the ideal which the body politic seeks.

An alternative approach based on economic theories of optimum behavior of households and businesses treats government as a decision-making unit that seeks to maximize the net benefits attained through

---

[1] Anthony Downs, *An Economic Theory of Democracy* (New York: Harper and Brothers, 1957), Chapter I.

[2] See Jerome Rothenberg, *The Measurement of Social Welfare* (Englewood Cliffs, New Jersey: Prentice-Hall, Inc., 1961), Chapter 11.

raising and spending public revenues. The body politic, in this view, does not aim at reelection but performs collective acts in a way that takes account of the individual preferences of all members of the community. Problems of ascertaining preferences and of giving equitable weights to divergent individual preferences when known make it impossible for any government to achieve the goal of utility maximization. Still, maximization of the sum of individual utilities is the basis of an economic model of government behavior, and allowance for diversity is the ideal of the economically oriented public body.

This study uses the economic model of government behavior because public spending primarily influences economic welfare, and a model based on economic rather than political principles seems appropriate. Further, reasoning from other areas of economics makes possible the application of theories and empirical results that are highly useful for developing a comprehensive logical framework for studying public spending. The formulation of a statistical model of the spending behavior of governments requires the establishment of a set of exhaustive categories into which all possible sources of variation among governmental units can be placed. The categories themselves can most effectively be established by applying the logic of maximization to indicate the relevant factors to be considered in decisions involving public spending. Then, with objective measures for the major elements in each category, the model can be tested.

In only a few of the studies discussed in the last chapter is there an attempt to develop a general explanation of public spending as a basis for selecting explanatory variables. For example, Brazer chooses independent variables on the basis of "logic . . . preliminary statistical analysis, as well as earlier studies." Scott and Feder start with twelve characteristics which they then reduce to six, entirely on statistical grounds. Hirsch does set up six broad categories of determinants but scarcely discusses the logic behind this procedure. McMahon is one of the few who spells out in terms of an over-all model why particular factors are included in his analysis.

A highly organized and integrated empirical model of the behavior of local schools, called the sequential simplex, has been developed over the years by Mort and his associates.[3] The model focuses on explaining the quality of the educational product in local school

<hr>

[3] The best brief description and explanation of the sequential simplex is in Paul R. Mort and Orlando F. Furno, *Theory and Synthesis of a Sequential Simplex* (New York: Institute of Administrative Research, Teacher's College, Columbia University, 1960).

systems defined by the number of, and speed of adoption of, certain educational practices. The factors that influence adaptations are grouped into five categories of varying directness in impact on the quality of education. This model does provide some insights into the interrelationship of changing educational goals and the spending necessary to achieve them. But factors explaining school spending and even the amount spent are used in the sequential simplex as independent variables that help to explain the quality of education. In this study school spending is the dependent variable to be explained by other factors. Mort's framework, therefore, is not appropriate.

THE GENERAL APPROACH

As background for the discussion of the step-by-step development of the empirical model, a brief overview of the study is presented here. The chief objective of the study is the identification of specific factors which are associated with different levels of educational expenditures made by the governments which directly administer public elementary and secondary education. The procedure is an analysis of educational expenditures during 1959-1960 in over 1,100 local school systems in 23 states. Expenditures are studied in relation to data about the schools themselves, the communities and states in which they are located, the interrelationship between state and local control and financing of education, and other relevant factors. The direction and magnitude of relationships are estimated by multiple regression.

The study is a cross-section analysis. It includes both dependent school systems in which municipalities and counties operate schools as one of many functions and independent school districts whose sole function is public education. The individual school system is the focus of the study because it is the decision-making unit. Aggregate levels of state or national expenditures are derived largely as a result of actions taken by the independent school boards and the city and county governments that maintain school systems. Cross-section analysis is used because changing boundaries and lack of year-by-year data for individual school systems make it impossible to obtain a series of observations that is adequate for statistical analysis. Further, unbiased estimates of relationships from time series require the dubious assumption of unchanging preferences.

Wide variations in legal and financial arrangements for administering public education among states dictate a procedure in which sources of variation in expenditures within states are distinguished from sources of variation among states. The approach used, therefore, consists of separate analyses of each individual state within the sample to determine the factors responsible for variations in expenditures among different school systems operating under similar state influences, as well as over-all analysis of all school systems in the sample regardless of location in which legal, financial, and other differences among the states are treated as independent variables.

DEVELOPMENT OF AN OPERATIONAL MODEL

If the maximization of community welfare is taken as the goal of public decision making in economic matters, then the logic and empirical methods used to study private economic decisions are relevant to a considerable extent in explaining government expenditures. The use of economic models of private decision making as a point of departure for an empirical model of educational spending involves three essential aspects. First, the dependent variable or variables must be determined. Second, a set of categories that reflects demand for education has to be derived from factors similar to those used by economists in empirical studies of expenditures for consumer goods. Third, another set of determinants of educational spending is needed that is based on factors which take into account estimates of costs and hence influence supply. In this study the concept of a set of all inclusive categories of independent variables based on models of private economic behavior underlies the methodology for the estimation of the determinants of public spending.

Selection of Dependent Variables

Capital versus Current Expenditures. In choosing the precise measure of expenditures to use in empirical studies of public spending a distinction must be drawn between current and capital outlays. Capital outlays by state and local governments are usually made when intensive use of existing facilities can no longer provide adequate levels of service. Government capital outlays, therefore, are irregular and may occur several years after an event which contributes to the need for them. Current expenditures, on the other hand, respond far more rapidly to year-by-year changes in the "needs" for services. For example, an increase in the number of pupils leads almost immediately to some increase in teaching staff, supplies used, and custodial and transportation services together with a probable increase in state aid payments to the school system. It may be several years, however, before enrollments increase sufficiently for a new school to be built.

Illustrations for factors other than enrollment growth could be presented. The point to be stressed is that decisions to spend for new public buildings and other capital outlays are based on quite different considerations from those determining levels of public expenditure for current operations.[4] Therefore, in this study of educational expenditures, as in other empirical studies of public spending, the analysis of current expenditures is separated from that of capital outlay.

Related to the decision to omit capital outlays is the further decision to exclude debt service, whether amortization or interest payments, from the dependent variable. The reason for this narrowing of the dependent variable so that it measures only current operating expenditures is that debt service as well as capital outlay reflect the influence of past events on local school spending. Since the analysis in the present study seeks to determine relationships between expenditures and current values of factors used as independent variables, expenditure elements determined by values of these factors which prevailed in previous periods would introduce unsystematic elements and confound the results. Outlays for amortization and interest on indebtedness do commit revenues of local school systems and thereby reduce funds available for operating expenditures. Debt service outlays, therefore, can be expected to influence the observed relationships between operating outlays and explanatory factors. As a consequence, the amount of debt service will be taken into account in the present study by treating it as an independent variable acting to reduce the amount of resources available for current operational expenditures.

The present study, then, includes only current operating expenditures, which constitute about 75 per cent of total expenditures on elementary and secondary education in the United States.

Omission of Public Spending for Higher Education. This study is narrowed further by the elimination of expenditures for state-supported colleges and universities and locally supported junior and community colleges. The reduction in scope is done to achieve "functional uniformity" among school systems and hence among the decision-making units studied. Only a few local school systems provide facilities for higher education. To include these expenditures as part of current

---

[4] The same argument for limiting expenditures to current outlays is given by Harvey E. Brazer in *City Expenditures in the United States* (New York: National Bureau of Economic Research, 1959), 2; and Joseph Berolzheimer, "Influences Shaping Expenditure for Operation of State and Local Governments," XXXII *National Tax Journal* (March 1947), 171.

educational outlays and then compare these outlays with current spending by school systems not providing higher education would confound any attempt to discover regularities in local school expenditure patterns. In the present study, then, the educational expenditures investigated are current operating expenditures administered by the officials of local school systems primarily for services to elementary and secondary school pupils.

The Dependent Variable as a Ratio. The most important element in explaining total current expenditures for elementary and secondary education is the number of children attending public schools. This number depends on the population within the area bounded by the school district, the proportion of school-age children in the population, and the extent to which nonpublic elementary and secondary educational facilities are used.

A statistical analysis of current educational spending would find population dominating other explanatory factors not only because of its importance in determining school enrollment but also because of its high correlation with other potential explanatory factors. This difficulty is usually circumvented by employing a per capita measure of expenditures as the dependent variable.[5] The total variance to be explained is reduced by the elimination of most of the effects of variation in population size. Studies of total expenditures usually explain far more variation than studies of per capita expenditures because in the former population size is so powerful an independent variable, while in the latter most of its effects have already been removed.

The use of per capita expenditures as a dependent variable has several implications. First, the magnitude of public expenditures for many purposes may depend largely upon the size of the population for whom the services are being performed. For example, the costs of a given level of police protection may vary directly with the number of persons to be protected. Using per capita expenditures as the dependent variable permits focusing on those factors which explain variations in the amount of services provided per unit of "need." In

[5] Studies of governmental expenditure employing per capita measures of public expenditures as the dependent variable include Brazer, *op. cit.*, and Berolzheimer, *op. cit.*; Stanley Scott and Edward L. Feder, *Factors Associated with Variations in Municipal Expenditure Levels* (Berkeley: Bureau of Public Administration, University of California, 1957); and Amos H. Hawley, "Metropolitan Population and Municipal Government Expenditure in Central Cities," 7 *Journal of Social Issues*, Nos. 1 and 2 (1951), 100-108. A recent study in which total rather than per capita expenditures is the dependent variable is Robert C. Wood, *1400 Governments* (Cambridge: Harvard University Press, 1961).

this context population is viewed as a quantitative measure of the need for services, and per capita expenditures may be considered a measure of quality of service provided.

A second implication of a per capita measure of expenditures is that it provides an estimate of the fiscal or financial burden of public spending. To an economist, concerned with the interrelationships among preferences, incomes, prices, governmental arrangements, and the use of scarce resources, per capita expenditures for a particular commodity or service is a revealing measure of the financial burden incurred in fulfilling certain needs. Comparison of per capita public expenditures shows the extent to which various communities are committing resources to particular functions and gives a measure of relative community effort provided by total current expenditures.

Studies of educational expenditures usually use expenditures per pupil as the "expenditure" variable. The chief reason for this treatment is that the number of pupils is a measure of need for educational services, and expenditure per pupil is a rough measure of the amount of such services provided. The strong interest of educators in per pupil expenditures and a desire to be able to compare this study with others are not the only arguments for including expenditures per pupil as an additional independent variable. Another reason is that not all school systems in the study operate both elementary and secondary schools. School district organization in some areas makes it impossible to adjust tuition transfers to estimate total expenditures for elementary and secondary education by those who reside in these incomplete systems. Where this situation occurs, the per capita expenditures of school systems that provide both elementary and secondary education must not be compared with those that include only one or the other. Per pupil expenditures, however, can be compared in such districts, although the level of schooling must be taken into account. In order to use information from these separate elementary or secondary districts, as well as to give an analysis on the basis of educational services provided, per pupil expenditures are included as another dependent variable in the study.

Distinguishing Locally Financed Expenditures. Local school systems obtain resources for financing current expenditures from grants-in-aid out of revenues collected by the state and federal governments and from revenues collected directly by the local school systems. Of course, a portion of state and federal grants-in-aid received by a school system comes from state and federal taxes levied on those living within its boundaries. Nevertheless, the revenues received from locally collected taxes for school purposes are determined by forces different from those shaping the amount of aid from state and federal governments. For example, the same factor may influence local tax receipts in one way and state aid in the opposite direction—as when low full property valuation per pupil means low local tax receipts but high state aid via an equalization formula. To differentiate these effects the study includes separate variables for total current operating expenditures and for current operating expenditures out of locally collected revenues (i.e., total current operating expenditures minus state and federal grants-in-aid). For convenience the latter variable will be called local expenditure.

Summary of Dependent Variables. The dependent variables in this study are based on two classifications of educational spending. One is the distinction between per pupil and per capita expenditure. The other is the difference between total expenditure and the amount of expenditure from locally raised revenues. In the analysis four separate dependent variables are used to reflect these classifications. These are: per capita total expenditure, per capita local expenditure, per pupil total expenditure, and per pupil local expenditure. In the analysis these dependent variables are used in parallel fashion and the nature and magnitude of the association of the independent variables to each of them is examined.

Selection of Independent Variables: General Remarks

The idea of a unit of commodity or service output in education probably cannot be objectively defined; still, the concept has conceptual meaning and use. The cost of a unit of educational output is the number of dollars it takes to provide educational services per pupil of equal quality in different communities. Larger expenditures attributable to the provision of different educational services represent quality differences and are not indications of higher cost. The quantity of educational services is probably best defined as the number of pupils enrolled in public schools. Although this definition has many drawbacks, in general the more pupils enrolled the greater the quantity of education provided.[6]

Studies of private spending for a commodity or service usually distinguish between those factors that influence demand and those that influence supply. Demand factors determine the number of units taken of a product of specified quality. Supply factors influence the per unit cost of the service or commodity and the differences in cost of products of varying quality. Total expenditures, of course, are

[6] See, in this series, William Wasserman, *Education Price and Quantity Indexes.*

equal to the number of units taken times the cost per unit of the particular quality product taken. In cross-section studies of the spending behavior of households only factors that influence demand are included because the cost of products depends on conditions confronting producers; the characteristics of individual households have nothing to do with these conditions. However, cross-section study of local spending for public education does require the inclusion of supply as well as demand factors because the local government both produces and consumes public education, and conditions in the community influence the cost of education as well as the demand for it. The explanatory variables used in this study are intended to reflect the underlying determinants of the quantity, cost, and quality of the educational services provided in individual school systems which, in turn, determine levels of expenditures.

Selection of Independent Variables: Demand Factors

Empirical study of household demand takes as its starting point a division of the determinants of demand into ability to buy, prices of commodities, and tastes or preferences of consumers. In cross-section studies of different consumer units at the same time, the prices facing all consumers are roughly the same and cannot account for variations in consumer spending. Most family budget studies use a measure of income as the major variable reflecting ability to pay, and wealth, usually in the form of liquid assets, often is included. Preferences or tastes are impossible to measure directly, but social and demographic characteristics can provide indications of preferences, especially for commodities whose consumption is closely related to family size and composition, or to socio-economic status. Spending behavior for most consumer units is not determined by a single individual but by some decision-making process in the family not yet fully identified by sociologists and social psychologists. Finally, certain consumer decisions are constrained by laws regarding zoning, public health, and other matters. Each of these categories—ability, preferences, characteristics of family decision-making, and legal constraints—are, or can be, represented by one or more specific factors that reflect sources of variation in demand among households.

The demand for public education, in this study, is viewed as being determined by essentially the same set of categories that have successfully been used in studies of household demand, although the specific variables representing them are somewhat different. It is believed that all possible sources of variation in demand for public education can be encompassed within the framework that follows.

Only variables thought to be important are actually included for consideration, however.

Ability to Spend. The most appropriate measure of ability to pay for education is probably the total income of the community in relation to its population. Personal and public debts are a deduction from these resources. The distribution of income and wealth is also important, as is the amount and form of wealth and the place of residence of its owners.[7]

Developing a measure or group of measures of local community ability to pay for public expenditures is more difficult than reflecting the income constraint of a consumer unit.[8] A danger that must be avoided is to identify tax receipts as the measure of ability. The tax-levying authority of a local government is quite important, and is discussed below. But the tax collections are generally determined jointly with anticipated levels of expenditures. Ability to pay is among the determinants of how much is collected and spent by public bodies, while tax collections are a measure of the extent to which ability to pay is used and not of the ability itself.

In the state-by-state analysis the variables reflecting positive ability to pay for current expenditures for education are median family income, the percentage of families with incomes of $10,000 or more, and the amount of equalized property value per capita when available. The amount of school debt service per capita is a measure of funds contractually committed to other purposes and is expected to be negatively related to spending.[9] In the over-all analysis of school systems, two statewide variables, personal income per capita and equalized value of property per capita, are included.

State and Federal Aid as Measures of Ability to Spend. Brazer and others who have studied public spending have included state and federal grants-in-aid for education as elements in ability to spend. While such funds certainly influence spending, they are not components of

---

[7] A persuasive argument that when a large proportion of wealth is owned by persons living outside the community effective tax rates tend to be higher is made in John J. Carroll and Seymour Sacks, "Local Sources of Local Revenue," *Proceedings of the Annual Conference on Taxation, 1961* (Harrisburg: National Tax Association, 1962), 294-311.

[8] Several indexes of taxpaying capacity of local governments have been developed. For example, see Advisory Commission on Intergovernmental Relations, *Measures of State and Local Fiscal Capacity and Tax Effort* (Washington, 1962).

[9] Ideally all contractual obligations of public revenues and private incomes by residents of the school system should be treated as offsets to ability to spend for education. Debt service on public school indebtedness, however, is the most important of these offsets in affecting current spending for local schools.

ability in the sense that income and property are. Grants-in-aid for education must be spent for education alone and are generally given directly in relation to the educational needs of a community and inversely in relation to its ability. These grants are spent dollar-for-dollar for education, and including them in a model does not explain school expenditures because they are, in fact, a component of expenditures. State and federal aid are reflected in this study by the effects of explanatory factors, such as property values and number of pupils, which are the underlying determinants of the amount of aid received. Furthermore, the effects of state and federal grants are taken into account by the two sets of dependent variables. One set includes total spending and the other deducts state and federal grants-in-aid to get a measure of locally raised expenditures. The same independent variables are related to the different dependent variables. Thus, different effects of the independent variables can be attributed to their relationship to state and federal aid.

The omission of state and federal aid to education as in independent variable is a major difference between this and other studies of local government spending. The omission of this factor probably reduces the proportion of variance explained by the final equation. But the variables included in this analysis go behind state and federal grants to the factors that determine them. To the extent that these intergovernmental grants are in themselves direct determinants of expenditures, this approach is deficient. However, the effects of grants-in-aid for education are primarily the consequence of the economic and demographic characteristics in local communities that determine the size of the intergovernmental payments. From this standpoint the method used in this study is superior because it estimates the effects of these community factors directly rather than through the intervening variable of state and federal aid.

Prices. Spending decisions by households depend upon the relative prices of consumer goods and services as well as on family incomes. Getting the most satisfaction from a given amount of income almost always requires that consumers buy more of an item when its price is lower. However, cross-section studies of demand exclude prices as an explanatory factor because most products are nationally marketed so that all consumer units generally face the same prices. Estimates of the responsiveness of consumer spending to changes in prices are obtained from time series analyses in which year-to-year changes in prices are a major explanatory variable. Regional variation in prices of commodities that are costly to transport are sometimes rather substantial, and if an adequate current index of regional prices were available for specific commodities it should, no doubt, be used in nationwide cross-section studies.

Since the cost of a given level of educational service is not the same in all communities, price differences are important in explaining variations in school system expenditures. Variations in the price of education result from differences in the costs of factors of production which schools need and which do not have nationally uniform prices, and from variations in the efficiency by which the school systems transform inputs into educational services. The elements which determine the costs of education are discussed below in the section dealing with the school system as a producing unit. The issue here is the effect of prices, however determined, on the demand for education.

Once determined, the cost or price of a given level of education influences the amount spent through its effect on demand. If education is relatively cheap in one community, more of it will be demanded and produced than in another community where preferences for education and ability to pay for it are the same but its cost greater. The demand relationship between quantity and price is an inverse one primarily reflecting the substitution of cheaper for costlier commodities as spenders attempt to get the most satisfaction from their limited resources. Educational spending can be expected to follow a similar pattern as communities substitute, to some extent, other public and private goods for education when its price is high in relation to other commodities, and vice versa when the price of educational service is relatively low. If regional differences in the cost of education can be specified, then an independent variable reflecting them should be included in the regression analysis.[10] The hypothetical relationship is that lower prices are associated with greater quantities of educational services. But the increase in quantity must be proportionately greater than the reduction in price if a greater amount of spending is to occur. The effect of price differences on total spending is most important, and specifying the magnitude of this relationship for public education, called the price elasticity of demand, would be extremely useful in anticipating the consequences of rising school costs.

An empirical estimate of the response to differences in costs re-

[10] If adjustments are made for regional differences in educational costs, it can be argued that regional variations in other costs as well should be taken into account. There are, however, no detailed regional price or cost indices available. Under these circumstances the use of a measure of variation in educational costs alone appears desirable, although it is an imperfect reflection of educational cost relative to all other costs.

quires a workable definition of educational output because price is associated inversely with quantity only for identical products. If lower prices prevail for a qualitatively inferior product, the quantity taken may be less than for a higher priced superior commodity. The figures chosen to represent the price of education in different school systems must, therefore, represent the price of a unit of educational service of uniform quality. While the over-all quality of education varies from one school system to another, it is probably true that the productivity of beginning teachers with undergraduate B.A. degrees is not greatly diverse. If so, an index of salaries paid to these crucial members of the school system is a good measure of educational cost because teachers' salaries comprise about 70 per cent of current expenditures, and salary scales tend to be proportional to beginning salaries. On the other hand, salary differentials among beginning teachers are not an appropriate measure of factor costs if differences in salaries reflect variations in productivity or in the length of the teaching day or year. In economic terms, the issue is whether spatial differences in rates of pay of teachers are predominantly the result of market imperfections or of differences in marginal productivity. Most salary differences among teachers appear to be the result of state and local financial circumstances coupled with strong preferences by teachers for particular geographical locations. An index of beginning teachers' salaries under these circumstances is a measure of the cost of obtaining a homogeneous input in various school systems. Further, this homogeneous input is presumed to yield rather similar outputs. The index of beginning salaries, then, is an approximate index of the relative costs among school systems of getting similar amounts of qualitatively equal educational outputs.

The view of the proper treatment of the cost of education in this study is entirely different from one that includes average teachers' salaries as an independent variable. Average salary is not a determinant of spending but the consequence of a decision about the quality of the educational services to be provided, based, probably, on preferences and capacity to pay. The approach used here includes an estimate of the cost of the most important single input of the school system and leaves the determination of the extent to which higher quality inputs are used to the other determinants of educational spending.

Preferences. With given incomes and prices, spending by a decision-making unit for a particular good or service depends upon its preferences. These preferences reflect what are commonly called needs, in the sense that larger families need more pairs of shoes or families with many children need more milk. In addition, the category of preferences encompasses the attitudes that influence choice among commodities that satisfy essentially similar needs; for example, with income and relative prices given, preferences determine whether a family buys a set of home appliances or hires a maid. Finally, preferences influence choices among quite disparate purchases, as when a family decides to forego a vacation to buy a new car. Because preferences cannot be measured objectively, economists treat them as a residual explanatory variable in the theory of consumer behavior. Behavior of family units that cannot be explained by variations in income and prices are attributed to preferences. A direct consideration of the effects of some preferences often can be achieved by grouping family units according to characteristics that are believed to be associated with preferences. Two-person family units are analyzed separately from units containing husband, wife, and children because there is agreement that the mix of goods needed in these different kinds of families is not the same. Many studies include objective measures of preferences as independent variables to obtain direct estimates of their effects. A variable for the weighted number of family members has long been used, and variables such as age, occupation, and education are frequently used as indications of preferences in analyses of consumer behavior.

Preferences for public education are similar in many respects to those for private goods and services. Given the legal requirement that the provision of public education is a responsibility of the state, and with the subsequent delegation of this power to a local government, there is no substitute for local public spending for education. Especially where the state mandates minimum expenditures or service levels in education, it is appropriate to talk of a need for educational outlays measured by the number of pupils to be educated. This minimum level is partly a reflection of statewide attitudes toward education. But the preferences of residents of specific local communities are likely to diverge from the state average. The role of preferences in determining expenditures beyond the mandated minimum depends on attitudes of the members of the local community, not only toward education but also toward other public services and private goods. Strong preferences for education, other things being equal, will raise school expenditures. But strong positive feelings about education must be weighed against such community needs as roads, sanitation, police and fire protection, as well as against needs for private consumption. An ideal set of independent variables reflecting these preferences would include measures of need for and attitudes toward education, other public and private goods, and personal savings. Also, existing stocks of public facilities such as school buildings and equipment, roads, sewers, playgrounds, and stocks of consumer durable goods such as homes, automobiles, and appliances would have to be taken into account. The more modest set of variables used in this study is intended to reflect objective needs for educational services and the attitudes of the members of the community toward education. No measures of stocks of public or private goods are included.

Direct need for educational services is measured in this study by the proportion of children under 18 in the population. An estimate for this variable is far more readily obtained than are figures for a more appropriate variable, the proportion of children 6 to 18. The proportion of children in the population is an estimate of total needs for education. The extent to which private and parochial schools reduce the need for public provision requires a second variable, the proportion of nonpublic school enrollment. Also, the per cent attending nonpublic schools may not only reduce per capita public school spending but per pupil spending as well if substantial use of private schools is associated with unfavorable attitudes toward public schools.

A variable included because it is believed to be positively associated with attitudes toward education is median years of schooling. The per cent of non-whites is included primarily to represent the lack of influence in the decision-making process of Negroes and other non-whites, but it may also be negatively related to spending because of low relative preferences for education by non-whites. As a cost factor, however, a large proportion of non-whites may be associated with higher expenditures, especially in school systems that maintain dual education systems or where delinquency is a concomitant of a relatively greater number of non-whites.

A final variable that may indicate negative attitudes toward education is the per cent of families that have moved into the school district within the past five years. Recent arrivals cannot vote for some time, often do not own property, and may not plan to be in the community long enough to derive benefits from higher outlays on education. On the other hand, expenditures will be higher if an influx of population reflects preferences for patterns of life in a community that includes a strongly supported local school system.

Independent Variables: Supply Factors

A public school system is a governmentally controlled production unit that combines factor inputs to provide educational outputs. The amount of spending in a particular school system depends on the costs of public education as well as on the demand for it. Considerations affecting the cost of services are complicated by the difficulty of distinguishing higher costs from higher quality. The cost of obtaining a given quality of educational services depends on two elements. First, there is the cost per unit of each of the inputs that the school system uses. While the cost of many inputs used by schools are identical, other costs such as salaries of equally trained teachers and wages paid to bus drivers and maintenance men vary widely even within the same state. Second, variations in cost occur because the efficiency with which inputs are transformed into outputs is not the same in all schools. In addition to variations in the determinants of the cost of a given quality of educational services, higher spending can result if different educational services are provided, causing quality to vary as well.

Cost of Inputs. A complete reflection of all the differences in the costs of inputs among schools would require variables showing the cost of a homogeneous unit of all factors used in providing education. Clearly such a set of variables is out of the question, and some simple measures of differences in the general cost of school inputs are needed. Since teachers' salaries comprise about 70 per cent of all current school spending, an index of the cost of a teacher of uniform skill in different school systems would be a rather good measure of costs. The variable that gives the salary of a beginning teacher with an undergraduate degree but no experience provides the desired index, if it is assumed that all teachers with similar training and experience are equally skilled, and that increments in salaries attributable to increased skills from further education and experience are proportional to initial salaries.

Treating the salaries of beginning teachers as a measure of differential input costs that affect the cost of education must be distinguished from viewing those same salaries as measures of the prices of educational outputs. In the former they are a measure of the cost of inputs and influence supply; in the latter use salaries are taken as measures of the price of a unit of output and influence demand. Usually units of output are measurable and have a demand price quite distinct from the cost of inputs. Units of service are not measurable and the cost of the service must be used as a proxy for the unit price of the output. Unfortunately, these circumstances make it impossible in this study to separate the effects of salary differences into price and cost influences, since the same variable signifies both elements. The effects of teachers' salaries must, therefore, be interpreted with caution.[11]

Although the cost of teachers is a dominant portion of current expenditures, differences in the prices of other factors can also lead to variations in spending. The proximity of a school system to an industrial or commercial center is likely to necessitate higher costs for many things that schools need. On the demand side, contact with a metropolitan center where the cultural and economic advantages of education are emphasized may have a favorable influence on local attitudes toward support for public schools. It is also possible that greater needs for other public and private goods and services in metropolitan areas act to reduce outlays for local schools. To represent these effects a variable classifying whether or not the school system is located in a standard metropolitan statistical area is included in the analysis.

Another factor on the cost side is transportation outlays. The amount of spending for transportation depends largely upon the distance covered and the numbers of pupils transported. Density is employed to provide a rough estimate of these varying costs of getting pupils to class.

Efficiency of Production. Production is the technical transformation of inputs into outputs, and the relationship that shows the largest number of units of output obtained from various combinations of inputs is the production function. Given the costs of the inputs, there are some combinations that yield output at lower costs per unit than other combinations, and the efficient producer uses the least-cost method of production. Private producers may use different methods of producing the same commodity, but the market tends toward uniform selling prices for identical products and elimination of inefficient producers. However, public education services are not purchased from private competitive producers and uniform prices do not prevail.

If output is of equal quality and factor costs are the same, what

---

[11] In a single estimating equation it is impossible to separate different aspects in which the same independent variable operates on the dependent variable. This difficulty, called the identification problem, arises at several points in the study. Occasionally it can be resolved by the use of highly complex multivariate statistical procedures. However, neither data nor theoretical knowledge in the area of the problem studied here are suitable for these complex methods. For a technical discussion of the identification problem and methods for resolving it see Lawrence R. Klein, *Econometrics* (Evanston, Illinois: Row, Peterson and Company, 1953), 17-18, 92-100.

characteristics will be associated with differences in school costs? One possibility, often investigated but seldom verified, is that economies are achieved once the school system reaches and exceeds a certain minimum size. These economies of scale occur primarily because increased specialization in larger school units makes possible the use of more efficient division of labor and other cost-reducing methods and equipment. The proper measure of the scale of school operation is not obvious, but over-all average daily attendance is most frequently used to indicate size. This simple variable is the one selected to test for economies of scale in this study.

The goods and services purchased by the current expenditures of a school system are not the only productive factors yielding educational outputs. School capital, including sites, buildings, and equipment, contribute to the product. If school capital is productive, it would be possible for a school system possessing a large amount of capital to provide a specified level of educational output with lower current outlays than those of a school system with less capital which must get more of its output from factors paid for out of current expenditures. To test this hypothesis, the insurable value of school capital per pupil is introduced into the regression as an explanatory variable. According to economic theory, schools having large amounts of capital will substitute it to a discernible extent for labor and other variable factors that require current expenditures. A difficulty in testing this hypothesis is that if larger amounts of school capital reflect positive attitudes toward public education or high levels of family income, its negative influence on outlays as a cost-reducing factor may be offset by these positive effects from the demand side.

Variations in Quality. The treatment of variations in quality is always difficult in empirical studies of spending, but these difficulties are especially severe for public services where qualitative differences are so hard to specify. In this study, for the most part variations in the quality of educational product among school systems are explained by the variables that reflect ability to pay and preferences for education. Thus, no variable such as average teachers' salaries is used to specify the quality of commonly provided educational services. There are, however, services provided in some school systems, such as preventive health check-ups, that are not undertaken in others, often because another governmental unit provides the service.

Quality variations are reduced considerably by excluding spending for both higher education and services to the community by local schools. The expenditures on the dependent variable are thus limited to those that are allocated to pupils. Still, there is considerable variation in the character of services performed in different schools. The services provided to secondary school pupils are more expensive than those to elementary pupils, and while these differences may be thought of as quantitative, they seem better classified as qualitative. The proportion of secondary attendance to total attendance is used here to represent the higher spending required to provide secondary education.

Another important dimension of quality is the number and extent of auxiliary services provided to school pupils. Services such as guidance, psychological counseling, and medical care are additional qualitative factors that are provided to pupils in some schools and not others. Spending for auxiliary services to others than pupils is excluded from the dependent variable, but failure to take account of those that are provided to pupils would omit a factor responsible for substantial variations in a few schools. To account for these differences, a measure of the number of such personnel per pupil is included among the explanatory variables and is expected to be positively associated with spending.

Selection of Independent Variables: Legal Constraints

State education laws limit the actions of public bodies that make ultimate decisions about local spending for education. These laws influence spending in two ways. They affect the cost and kind of school services provided by specifying standards of input quality and characteristics of the curriculum. Also, state aid regulations influence the effectuation of demand for education by limitations on the taxing and borrowing powers of local governments. State laws thus determine the capacity to tap local ability to pay.

Differences in legal provisions facing school boards or their counterparts in dependent school systems exist within, as well as among states. In most states there are several classifications of school systems, and often different legal regulations apply to each type. It is difficult to incorporate into the analysis explanatory variables that reflect differences in legal requirements that affect spending directly, by influencing grants-in-aid or mandated tax levies, or indirectly by determining the nature of the local decision-making process.

With one exception, differences in legal and decision-making characteristics within states are not treated in this study. The analysis does not consider factors such as supplementary taxing powers granted to larger cities in some states, or the ability to borrow without referendum given to certain school districts in a state. The variables included reflect legal characteristics for an entire state and therefore do not vary for intrastate school systems. The sole exception is fiscal dependence or independence. In states where both patterns are found, individual school systems have been classified accordingly and an explanatory variable for this factor is included in the state-by-state regressions.

State Aid. State grants to local schools are generally classified according to whether they are flat or equalizing grants and whether they are general or specific purpose grants. Equalizing grants often are based on measures of local fiscal capacity relative to the number of pupils enrolled in public schools. Flat grants, on the other hand, are not related to the financial position of the local school and typically depend on the numbers of pupils per classroom. Apart from the criteria for determining the amounts given to local schools, state grants can be mandated for specific purposes, such as teachers' salaries or language and science programs, or the grants can be general purpose ones that are used as the local school sees fit.

Although most states extend all four types of aid, usually one type predominates. Different forms of state aid are thought to have different impacts on the amount of locally raised revenues for schools. In addition, the proportion of total current spending for education in a state that comes from state grants is likely to be associated with differences in spending among states.

To reflect differences in state aid patterns among states, three explanatory variables are introduced into the computations that include school systems in different states. One variable is the statewide ratio of locally collected revenues to total revenues for local schools. The other two are general purpose grants and equalizing grants as percentages of total state grants for local schools. These three variables are identical for all school systems in a given state and are intended to reflect over-all state aid arrangements. They do not portray the amount or proportion of state aid going to particular school systems, and hence are not subject to objections raised to the inclusion of intergovernmental revenues as independent variables.

State and Local Taxing Powers. The ability of a local or state government to spend for any public function ultimately depends on the income and wealth of the area. To tap these resources, however, requires powers to tax which are not always granted. Without specifying the taxing powers of each individual school system, it was anticipated that the proportion of total state and local tax receipts from taxes other than those on property would be a satisfactory measure of tax flexibility. The hypothesis was that lessened reliance on the property tax is associated with increased opportunities to tap existing income and wealth and thus should be positively related to spending. However, preliminary analysis revealed a negative correlation of over .90 between the proportion of revenues from nonproperty taxation and state revenues as a fraction of total revenues for local schools. Two independent variables with this high an intercorrelation should not be included in the same equation, and therefore the proportion of revenue from nonproperty taxes was eliminated from the final analysis.

The Local Decision-Making Process. Ultimately it is the local body politic that makes the final decision regarding the amount of local school spending. To be sure, this decision-making body is constrained by the forces that make up the demand for education in the community it represents and the factor costs and technological conditions that determine the outlays necessary for various qualities of educational services. At the same time, state regulations must be adhered to and opportunities for state and federal grants taken into account. Still, the decision is far from being determined by these factors alone.

For two reasons it is difficult to specify variables that differentiate decision-making units in accordance with the amounts they spend. Conceptually, it is not clear what characteristics of public bodies are likely to be associated with differences in their spending decisions. Technically, getting a set of comparable nationwide data is a substantial task in itself because the method of selection and the powers of school boards vary both within and among states. Several other studies in this project are specifically directed toward this problem in local school systems.[12]

Included here is only the simplest and most obvious single characteristic of the decision-making body, its dependence on or independence of other governments in the final decision regarding expenditures. It has been argued that in independent school districts decisions are ultimately voter-controlled and therefore no higher governmental check is needed. Where voters do not vote directly on school expenditures a check is necessary and dependent school systems are found. If this argument is correct, the variable reflecting the independent

[12] See the monographs in this series by Warner Bloomberg, Jr. and Morris Sunshine, *Suburban Power Structures and Public Education;* and Roscoe C. Martin, *Government and the Suburban School.*

character of the school system is also a measure of the effect of more direct voter participation in school financing. Margolis contends that dependent systems permit trading among public projects that benefit different segments of the community.[13] He suggests that possibilities for trading may lead to higher spending on all functions. It is this hypothesis that is tested by the variable for dependence.[14]

THE SAMPLE

A statistical analysis leading to the identification of major factors associated with variations in spending by local school systems requires data from different systems within a given state and from systems in different states. To be useful for such an analysis the sample must include an adequate number of school systems within a particular state to permit the use of a multivariate statistical technique. At the same time, school systems in a sufficiently large number of states must be sampled so that variables associated with systematic differences in expenditures among states can be identified.

The essence of any sampling problem is the determination of how many units to sample and in what proportion to sample them from different strata. This is a problem because financial resources for research are limited, and usually the researcher can select for systematic study only a portion of the universe with which he is dealing. Subject to the constraints imposed by financial considerations, the sampling statistician tries to select the most efficient sample design for estimating the values of those parameters of the population in which he is interested. The objective in choosing among sample designs is to select the one which yields the least variance (i.e., the most precision, the most information) per unit cost.[15]

Limitations of funds and research personnel made it impossible in this study to start with a population of over 42,000 school systems and apply principles of scientific sampling to the selection of an optimum sample. Fortunately, the Office of Education, with the assist-

---

[13] Julius Margolis, "Metropolitan Finance Problems: Territories, Functions, and Growth," in *Public Finances: Needs, Sources, and Utilization* (Princeton: National Bureau of Economic Research, 1961), 261-66.

[14] Table 2, in Chapter V, summarizes the dependent and independent variables discussed in this chapter.

[15] These comments on efficient sample design are adapted from Leslie Kish, "Selection of the Sample," in Leon Festinger and Daniel Katz, eds., *Research Methods in the Behavioral Sciences* (New York: Dryden Press, 1953).

ance of the sampling statisticians of the Bureau of the Census, has recently completed the selection of a sample of approximately 8,000 school systems stratified by state and by size of school system within states. In the Office of Education sample the parameter whose variance is minimized per unit of cost is current expenditures per pupil classified by geographical region and by enrollment-size group. The Office of Education's sample is probably as efficient for this study as any sample based on estimating a single parameter in the area of educational finance.[16]

The costs of data collection and analysis of a sample of 8,000 school systems in all states, however, were too large for the resources available here. Estimation of the costs of analysis and data collection indicated that approximately 1,700 individual school systems could be sampled within the limits of the resources available. Furthermore, preliminary study showed that from 50 to 60 observations per state were needed for satisfactory application of the multivariate techniques required to explain within state variations in local school expenditures. To get 50 to 60 returns from a mail questionnaire sent to school superintendents who had already responded to a similar mail questionnaire from the Office of Education it was estimated that initially about 80 school systems would have to be selected. With 80 school systems per state and about 1,700 as a total, the number of states which could be included was about 21. The total number of states selected was increased to 23, however, because a few states in the South have countywide school systems with far fewer than 80 independent operating school systems. With proper selection this number of states is sufficient to test hypotheses regarding the effects on local school expenditures of the different financial and administrative arrangements that exist between local school governments and individual states.

The 23 states were chosen by stratifying on the basis of both the

[16] There is a major problem in determining an optimum sample design for estimating more than one parameter from any given sample. In this situation there are as many variances as there are parameters to be estimated, and a sample design which minimizes the variance of one parameter may result in other parameters with large variances. This problem can be solved, theoretically, if relative weights are assigned to the variables indicating the importance to the researcher of minimizing the different variances. Usually, however, the purpose of a multivariate study is precisely to discover the relative importance of the different variables and, hence, it is impossible to specify beforehand which variances should be minimized.

character of the state aid program and the size of public school enrollment. After several alternative classifications were tried, it was decided that the presence or absence of statewide property equalization for state aid purposes was the best rough and ready device for stratifying state aid schemes. This stratification technique provided a selection of states which reflected the range of economic and social differences among states as well as the different patterns of relationships between state governments and local school systems. The 48 continental states were then divided into two groups, those with property equalization and those without. Then, within each of these groups, states were selected by a random process in which each state had a probability of being selected in accordance with its public school enrollment.

Within almost all of the states selected there were far more than 80 individual school systems in the Office of Education's sample. As a way of cutting down the number of observations in each state and also of making those school systems included in this study more uniform in character, all school systems of fewer than 300 pupils were dropped from the analysis. As a consequence, the results of this study can be generalized only for school systems of over 300 pupils. The reduction in comprehensiveness as a consequence of this omission is small, however, amounting to only 4 per cent of pupils enrolled and probably an even smaller proportion of current operating expenditures.

After reducing the number of school systems within the selected states by eliminating those with 300 pupils or less, the number of systems remaining was still in excess of 80 in many states. The reduction to 80 was accomplished by ascertaining the ratio of selection which would reduce the remainder to 80 (e.g., if there were 160 school systems remaining the ratio is 1/2) and then selecting those school systems to be included by a random choice (e.g., taking every second one from an alphabetical listing by size class).

The result is a sampling of states superimposed on a subsample of the Office of Education's sample of school systems within states. The probability of any particular state's falling into the initial sample can be determined; it depends upon whether it has statewide property equalization and upon its public school enrollment. The probability that any particular school system in a selected state will be in the sample is also determinate, being equal to the product of its sampling ratio in the Office of Education's sample and the ratio by which the redundant school systems in a given state were reduced to 80. The total probability that any school system will be in the sample, then, is the product of the probability of the state being in the sample and of the individual school system being in the state sample.

The response rate, measured in terms of usable questionnaires, was about 65 per cent. In view of the nature of the data requested and the demands on school finance officers, this rate is quite high. Still, the number of nonresponses may be sufficient to impair significantly the representativeness of the school systems that remain in the analysis. Since the study aims at estimating relationships rather than mean values for specific variables, the effects of a nonrepresentative sample cannot be stated precisely. Clearly, the results must be treated as provisional and emphasis placed on comparability among states rather than on conventional measures of statistical significance. If confidence intervals are employed conservative standards are required.

THE DATA

Data for the variables used in the study come primarily from three sources. The first is an original questionnaire sent to school superintendents covering the geographical location of the school system, the population residing within its boundaries, salaries of beginning teachers, the value of school buildings and equipment, and the value of property taxable for school purposes. Second, financial and enrollment figures come from data provided by the U.S. Office of Education's questionnaire survey of *Statistics of Local Public School Systems for the School Year 1959-1960*. Third, the social, economic, and demographic characteristics of communities are derived from the 1960 Decennial Census. Sources for statewide variables include *Revenue Programs for the Public Schools in the United States 1959-1960* and issues of the *Survey of Current Business*.

Only the data for community characteristics derived from census materials presented unusual difficulties. While figures for other variables unquestionably are subject to errors, they do pertain directly to the school system or state being studied and there are no superior sources of data available. Census data, however, required special treatment because they are presented for governmental units which often are not coterminous with school system boundaries. The determination of figures for median family income, proportion of school-age children and similar characteristics was straightforward for countywide and municipal school systems whose boundaries do coincide with units reported in the Census. To obtain estimates of these variables for noncoterminous systems an extension of procedures developed by urban sociologists was used. School districts were classified according to the census unit which most reflected their circumstances. For example, suburbs located in urban fringe areas were assigned the values of the over-all urban fringe, and those in rural areas were given values for the county less urban places within the county.[17] It is believed that this procedure on the whole assigns relatively accurate values. Insistence on great accuracy in these measures of the characteristics of local communities would have permitted the inclusion of only coterminous systems with consequent reduction in the scope of the study and the generality of its conclusions.

METHOD OF ANALYSIS

Fulfilling the objectives of this study requires specifying the effects of various influences upon levels of local school expenditures. In this chapter, the complexity of the determination of such expenditures has been described, and it is clear that only by means of a multivariate statistical technique will it be possible to estimate the desired "net" effects. Simpler techniques would lead to a situation where null hypotheses regarding specific factors could seldom be rejected; nor could positive hypotheses be supported, because failure to consider some crucial factor might bias the analysis.

Modern statistical methods offer a number of multivariate techniques, each intended for somewhat different circumstances. This study aims at determining the factors systematically associated with variations in local school expenditures and, at the same time, with estimating the magnitude, direction, and importance of the effect of these factors. These statistical objectives dictate an estimation statistic (such as multiple regression) rather than a test statistic (such as multivariate analysis of variance) which estimates the probability that the values of certain parameters are truly different.[18] Although there are several multivariate estimating techniques in addition to least-squares regression, this particular technique requires the least

[17] A detailed description of the methods used to obtain estimates of social and economic characteristics for noncoterminous school systems will be provided upon request by the Project for Research in Educational Finance, Maxwell Graduate School, Syracuse University.

[18] The distinction between an estimation and a test statistic is developed in Keith Smith, "Distribution-free Statistical Methods and the Concept of Power Efficiency," in Festinger and Katz, eds., *op. cit.*, 537-38.

restrictive assumptions about the nature of the variables to provide unbiased estimates of parameters. Also, it is easily programmed for use on high-speed computers, and its results are relatively easy to interpret. For these reasons, the major method of analysis used is least-squares multiple regression.

V. Results of the Analysis

THIS CHAPTER presents the results of the study of the determinants of current expenditures by local school systems. The statistical analysis consists of estimates of simple and partial correlation coefficients and least-squares multiple-regression equations for each of the four dependent variables. These correlations and regression equations are estimated both for all school systems taken together and separately in each of 21 states.[1] The results of the regressions are shown by net regression coefficients and beta coefficients. Although tests of statistical significance have only limited applicability, those coefficients significant at the .95 level of probability, according to conventional criteria, have been footnoted in the tabular material. Comparison of results among states and among variables, however, dominates the evaluation of findings.

METHOD OF PRESENTATION

To aid in the interpretation and presentation of results, Table 2 provides a description of all variables used in the study and of the units in which they are measured. This table is needed to interpret the net regression coefficients which indicate the effect of a change of one unit of an independent variable on the number of dollars of current expenditure for public education. The magnitudes of the net regression coefficients depend largely on the units in which the independent variables are measured. The standardized regression coefficient, or, as it is sometimes called, the beta coefficient, is a statistic that makes it possible to compare the relative importance of regression coefficients for different independent variables. Beta coefficients measure the effect of a variation of one standard deviation in an independent variable on the standard deviation of the dependent variable. Thus the beta coefficient measures the relative contribution of each of the independent variables to the explanation of the dependent variable in the context of the over-all multivariate regression equation.

[1] Separate analyses of Maryland and Delaware were precluded by an insufficient number of observations.

TABLE 2

DEFINITIONS OF VARIABLES AND SOURCES OF DATA

Variables	Units	Abbreviations
DEPENDENT VARIABLES:		
1. Total Current Expenditures Per Capita*	$	(TE/C)
2. Local Expenditures Per Capita (total current expenditures minus state and federal aid)†	$	(LE/C)
3. Total Current Expenditures Per Pupil‡	$	(TE/P)
4. Local Expenditures Per Pupil†,‡	$	(LE/P)
INDEPENDENT VARIABLES:		
Variables Reflecting Demand Elements		
5. Median Family Income**	$	(Y)
6. Per Cent of Families with Income of $10,000 or more**	%	(Y+)
7. Amount of Equalized Property Value Per Capita††	$	(PROP)
8. Amount of Debt Service Per Capita††	$	(DS)
9. Statewide Personal Income Per Capita‡‡	$	(Y/C)
10. Statewide Equalized Value of Property Per Capita***	$	(PROP/C)
11. Salary of Beginning Teachers††	$	(SAL)
12. Per Cent of Children Under 18**	%	(CHILD)
13. Per Cent of Children in Non-Public Schools**	%	(PRIV)
14. Median Years of Education**	years	(ED)
15. Per Cent Non-White**	%	(NON-W)
16. Per Cent Moved into District in Last Five Years**	%	(MIGR)
Variables Reflecting Supply Elements		
11. Salary of Beginning Teachers (see 11 above)††	$	(SAL)
17. Located in Standard Metropolitan Statistical Area**	0 or 1	(SMSA)
18. Density††	persons per sq. mile	(DEN)
19. Number of Pupils in Average Daily Attendance†	pupils	(ADA)
20. Insurable Value of School Capital Per Pupil††	$ per ADA	(CAP)
21. Per Cent of Pupils in Secondary Grades†	%	(SEC)
22. Number of Full Time Employees in Auxiliary Services Per Pupil†,†††	per ADA	(AUX)
Variables Reflecting Legal Differences Among States		
23. Dependent or Independent School System††	0 or 1	(DEP)
24. State Collected Revenues/Total Revenues for Education**	%	(SR/TR)
25. Equalization Aid/Total State Aid for Education†††	%	(EA/TA)
26. General Purpose Aid/Total State Aid for Education†††	%	(GPA/TA)

With certain adjustments beta coefficients can be summed to provide an allocation of the total explained variance among the independent variables. The partial correlation coefficient, on the other hand, measures the association of the dependent variable with a single independent variable when the effects of all other independent variables have been held constant. It is a measure of the net correlation of an independent variable with the dependent variable. The sum of the partial correlations has no special significance.[2]

Before turning to a discussion of the findings, three aspects of the data should be mentioned. First, as the footnotes to Table 2 indicate, expenditure data used in this study come from a questionnaire survey administered by the U.S. Office of Education. Figures for local current expenditures were obtained by subtracting state and federal aid from total current expenditures. However, in responses of local school offi-

---

[2] See Frederic C. Mills, *Statistical Methods*, 3rd ed. (New York: Henry Holt and Company, 1955), 631-45, for a technical discussion of net regression, beta, and partial correlation coefficients.

---

* Current expenditures are from *Statistics of Local Public School Systems for the School Year 1959-60*, a questionnaire administered by the U.S. Office of Education. Current expenditures include: Administration; Instruction; Attendance Services; Health Services; Pupil Transportation Services; Operation and Maintenance of Plant; and Fixed Charges.

Population is from replies to a questionnaire sent to local school superintendents.

† Local expenditures are determined from responses to the U.S. Office of Education's questionnaire by subtracting the amount of state and federal aid received from the total current expenditures of each school system.

‡ Figures for average daily attendance from the U.S. Office of Education's questionnaire are used as the denominator to obtain per pupil expenditures.

** Estimated from figures in U.S. Bureau of the Census, *United States Census of Population: 1960. Number of Inhabitants*, Series A, volumes by states (Washington, 1961), 17, Table 10; U.S. Bureau of the Census, *United States Census of Population: 1960. General Population Characteristics*, Series B, volumes by states (Washington, 1962), variable 12, Tables 13, 20, 22, 23, 24 or 25; variable 15, *ibid.*; U.S. Bureau of the Census, *United States Census of Population: 1960. General Social and Economic Characteristics*, Series C, volumes by states (Washington, 1962), variables 5, 6, 13, 14, 16, Tables 33, 34.

†† Data are from replies to the questionnaires administered as part of this study, plus occasional reference to publications of state departments of education.

‡‡ *Survey of Current Business* (August 1962).

*** Based on estimates of equalized property values among states in U.S. Bureau of the Census, *Taxable Property Values in the United States* (Washington, 1957), 22.

††† U.S. Office of Education, *Revenue Programs for the Public Schools in the United States, 1959-60*, (Washington, 1961), 7, 12, 13.

‡‡‡ Auxiliary services includes persons in health, medical, psychological, and guidance services. Data secured from the questionnaire to school superintendents.

cials, based on the standard receipt and expenditure accounts recommended by the Office of Education, the local school systems include funds received for capital as well as current expenditures as part of state and federal aid. Although aid for capital outlays is a relatively small portion of total aid, its inclusion distorts the actual measure of local current expenditures from what is conceptually desired. The difficulty here is that when state grants for capital outlays are deducted from total current expenditures, the resulting figure understates local current expenditures. There is, unfortunately, no way of measuring these effects within the limits of the data available.

Second, the data for median family income, proportion of children in the population, and the other measures of local economic and social characteristics were derived from census data by an unverified process and are subject to error.[3] No attempt is made in the discussion that follows to attribute any of the results to errors in these underlying data, and there is no reason to believe that systematic bias has occurred. Nonetheless, it is not impossible that errors in the data influence, to some extent, the parameter estimates. Third, the results apply only to medium and large systems because of the omission from the sample of school systems with fewer than 300 pupils.

COMBINED ANALYSIS OF ALL SCHOOL SYSTEMS IN THE SAMPLE

The over-all analysis of all school systems in the sample encompasses 20 independent variables.[4] Of these, 15 vary among all school systems while 5 are statewide measures that vary only among systems in different states. Among the school systems in this nationwide sample, the variability of per pupil expenditures for public elementary and secondary education is greater than that for per capita expenditures and variability for local spending greater than for total spending. But, as Table 3 shows, regression equations of identical form generally explain a higher portion of variance for those dependent variables that have the largest coefficients of variability.

Simple Correlations

Although multivariate analysis is required to test the hypotheses developed in the previous chapter, some interest may attach to the

---

[3] The procedure is discussed in Chapter IV. See also footnote 17, Chapter IV.

[4] Debt service is excluded because data were not obtained for all states. Equalized property valuations are available for only six of the states included in the study.

TABLE 3

GENERAL CHARACTERISTICS OF THE OVER-ALL ANALYSIS

Dependent Variable	Mean of Dependent Variable	Coefficient of Variability*	Multiple Regression Coefficient	Number of Observations
TE/C	$ 64.11†	.502	.558	884
LE/C	$ 32.29	.828	.689	880
TE/P	$346.61‡	.721	.735	1127
LE/P	$189.58	1.057	.780	1041

* Defined as standard deviation/mean.
† A figure of $68.14 for direct per capita noncapital expenditures for all fifty states and the District of Columbia is given in *Governmental Finances in 1960*, U.S. Bureau of the Census (Washington, 1960), 33.
‡ A figure of $345 for per pupil current expenditures is obtained by dividing expenditures from *ibid.*, 32, and enrollment from *Public School Systems in 1960*, U.S. Bureau of the Census (Washington, 1960), 1.

simple correlation coefficients between the independent variables and each of the four dependent variables.[5] The first part of Table 4 shows that all of the measures of ability to pay have positive correlations, and while none has an overwhelming influence, all are substantial. The correlations of proportion of children in the population are negative, and those for per cent in nonpublic schools and per cent migrant are both positive. It may be noted that these findings are at odds with the presumed direction of their influence. The negative correlations for proportion of non-white, however, are as expected.

Most of the factors that represent cost elements have positive correlation coefficients: salary of beginning teachers, proportion in secondary grades, and location in a Standard Metropolitan Statistical Area. Of all variables, the number of persons employed in the provision of auxiliary services is most highly correlated with both categories of per pupil expenditures. Density, average daily attendance, and amount of school capital have, in general, low positive correlation coefficients. Larger state participation in the collection of revenues for local schools has a negative influence. This, however, may be attributed to the fact that poorer states generally tend to shift a larger proportion of revenue collection for schools to the state level. (See Table A.1.) These complex relationships are further examined below. The correlation of the two variables that indicate alternative bases for state grants-in-aid are small and irregular.

In addition to an over-all examination of the simple correlations, it

[5] Appendix Table 1 contains a matrix of intercorrelations among the independent variables for all school systems in the sample.

TABLE 4
SIMPLE AND PARTIAL CORRELATIONS AND NET AND STANDARDIZED
REGRESSION COEFFICIENTS FOR ALL SCHOOL SYSTEMS IN THE SAMPLE*

DEP. VAR.	Y	Y+	Y/C†	PROP/C†	CHILD	PRIV	ED	NON-W	MIGR	SAL	DEN
					INDEPENDENT				- - - - - -		
			SIMPLE CORRELATION COEFFICIENTS								
TE/C	.21	.29	.42	32	.00	.09	.14	-.22	.05	.39	-.02
LE/C	.43	.55	.57	.42	-.25	.41	.31	-.41	.06	.54	.18
TE/P	.25	.28	.37	.25	-.15	.25	.17	-.24	.01	.35	.19
LE/P	.37	.44	.43	.28	-.25	.42	.25	-.31	-.01	.43	.28
			HIGHEST ORDER PARTIAL CORRELATION COEFFICIENTS								
TE/C	-.05	.13‡	.28‡	.02	.17‡	-.09‡	-.02	.01	-.05	.15‡	-.06
LE/C	.01	.26‡	.06	.03	.03	.04	-.01	.05	-.03	.04	-.01
TE/P	.00	.01	.05	-.03	.00	.03	.00	.00	-.03	.04	.02
LE/P	.02	.15‡	-.12‡	-.01	-.06	.10‡	-.01	.06	-.03	.01	.07‡
			NET REGRESSION COEFFICIENTS								
TE/C	-.07	.53‡	3.48‡	.08	1.16‡	-.25‡	-.30	.03	-.16	1.23‡	-.06
LE/C	.01	.80‡	.52	.07	.17	.08	-.10	.08	-.07	.22	-.01
TE/P	-.03	.16	3.62	-.06	.19	.51	-.32	.02	-.57	2.01	.17
LE/P	.15	2.74‡	-7.11‡	-.18	-1.77	1.39‡	-.50	.66	-.48	.38	.35‡
			STANDARDIZED REGRESSION COEFFICIENTS								
TE/C	-.05	.17‡	.49‡	.03	.17‡	-.10‡	-.02	.01	-.04	.23‡	-.06
LE/C	.01	.33‡	.09	.03	.03	.04	-.01	.05	-.02	.05	-.01
TE/P	.00	.01	.07	-.03	.00	.02	.00	.00	-.02	.05	.02
LE/P	.02	.16‡	-.17‡	-.01	-.04	.09‡	-.01	.05	-.02	.01	.06‡

								GPA	
ADA	CAP	SEC	AUX	SMSA	DEP	SR/TR†	EA/TA†	TA†	CONSTANT
SIMPLE CORRELATION COEFFICIENTS									
-.05	.05	.16	.20	.10	-.11	-.26	.06	.08	
.00	-.01	.17	.29	.31	.04	-.60	-.01	-.07	
.01	.00	.16	.71	.20	-.01	-.28	.00	.07	
.03	.02	.19	.67	.28	.06	-.48	-.04	-.03	
HIGHEST ORDER PARTIAL CORRELATION COEFFICIENTS									
-.03	-.05	.10‡	.05	-.11‡	-.08‡	.11‡	.05	.02	
-.02	-.05	.07‡	.09‡	-.05	-.03	-.22‡	.00	-.04	
.01	-.07‡	.04	.66‡	.03	-.09‡	-.02	-.03	.13‡	
.00	-.06	.09‡	.63‡	.05	-.04	-.26‡	-.07‡	.07‡	
NET REGRESSION COEFFICIENTS									
.00	.00	.30‡	.71	-7.44‡	-6.06‡	.32	.05	.03	-125.02
.00	.00	.14‡	1.02‡	-2.79	-1.57	-.48	.00	-.03	11.57
.00	-.02‡	.35	81.79‡	14.14	-43.26‡	-.26	-.19	.98‡	14.25
.00	-.01	.65‡	55.15‡	1.44	-1.40	-3.54‡	-.32‡	.39‡	364.67
STANDARDIZED REGRESSION COEFFICIENTS									
-.03	-.04	.09‡	.04	-.12‡	-.09‡	.19‡	.05	.05	
-.02	-.03	.05‡	.08‡	-.05	-.03	-.34‡	.00	-.03	
.01	-.05‡	.03	.66‡	.03	-.08‡	-.02	-.02	.10‡	
.00	-.04	.06‡	.55‡	.04	-.03	-.34‡	-.05‡	.05‡	

* See Table 2 for an explanation of abbreviations and a description of variables.
† Variable differs from state to state, but is constant for all school systems within a state.
‡ Significant at .95 level of probability under assumptions of simple random sampling, homogeneous variances, and other conditions for the application of conventional confidence intervals.

is useful to examine variations in the coefficients for the same independent variable in the different expenditure categories. Such an examination shows that for both per capita and per pupil expenditures the coefficients for local outlays consistently exceed those for total outlays. This pattern of stronger association between local expenditures and measures of local characteristics indicates that state and federal aid tend to even out total expenditures. These correlations constitute another illustration of the relatively lower variability of total expenditures which is shown directly by the coefficients of variability of Table 3.

Multivariate Analysis

The highest order partial correlation coefficients, which estimate the relationship of each independent variable to the dependent variable when all other independent variables are taken into account, are, on the whole, considerably lower than the simple correlations. For several variables the signs of the coefficients of partial correlation are opposite to those of simple correlation. The standardized regression coefficients reveal that for few of the independent factors is there covariation of as much as 25 per cent expressed in standard deviation units of the dependent variable.

Per Capita Expenditures. The levels of state per capita income are the most important positive determinant of total per capita expenditures. The extent to which the state participates in the collection of revenues for local schools is also significant. Median family income in local communities is, if anything, a negative factor, but the proportion of families with incomes of $10,000 or more and the proportion of children in the population both are associated with higher total expenditures. The proportion in private schools has a negative effect. Among factors that reflect local costs, the proportion of pupils in secondary grades and the salary of beginning teachers tend to raise total expenditures. Location in a Standard Metropolitan Statistical Area and dependent school district organization both have negative effects on total spending.

Local per capita expenditures are negatively related to the extent of state participation in school revenue collections and positively associated with measures of local income. Cost factors are less important for local than for total expenditures, as are location and organization, although both the proportion in secondary grades and the provision of more extensive health and counseling services have a positive influence on local spending per capita.

Per Pupil Expenditures. Auxiliary services are the most important determinant of both total and local per pupil expenditures; the partial correlation coefficients of .66 and .63 for this variable are almost as high as the simple correlations. There is no evidence that total expenditures per pupil are affected in a systematic way by local demand or cost factors or by state personal income and participation in the finance of local schools, although a larger proportion of general rather than special-purpose aid is associated with slightly higher per pupil outlays. Local expenditures, however, respond positively to local variables such as the proportion of families with incomes of $10,000 or more, higher relative secondary school enrollment, and density, and negatively to state personal income and to a greater proportion of revenues for local schools collected by the state.

An Interpretation of the Findings. An imperfect but discernible pattern emerges from these regressions and partial correlation coefficients. Differences between coefficients for total and local expenditures appear to stem primarily from the nature of state provisions for grants-in-aid to local schools. As a consequence of efforts to provide some degree of equalization, such aid generally is granted inversely to local ability to pay and directly with conditions that indicate higher costs. These arrangements result in a pattern in which the contribution to educational expenditures by the local community varies moderately in accordance with its ability to pay and the costs of the quantity and quality of the services provided. Total expenditures, however, are affected strongly by grants-in-aid based on various formulas for the equalization of educational services among school systems within a state, thus reducing the influence of local factors. The statistical analysis shows that in contrast to local expenditures, total expenditures vary directly in proportion to the economic capacity of the state, the relative number of children to be educated in local schools, the proportion of pupils in secondary schools, and the salary level of beginning teachers, and are inversely related to density, dependent school organization, and location in a Standard Metropolitan Statistical Area.

These generalizations can be illustrated by a comparison of net regression and partial correlation coefficients in the four equations. A low correlation or regression coefficient for an independent variable in one of the equations for total expenditures indicates that these expenditures do not vary greatly among school systems with different values for the factor in question. If the same factor has a higher regression coefficient in the corresponding equation for local expenditures, there is evidence that state aid has acted to equalize the impact of this variable on total spending by granting aid in a way that has an effect inverse to the influence of the variable on local expenditures.

These relationships are reversed when the regression coefficient for total expenditures exceeds that for local expenditures. Higher local incomes, for example, do not have a strong positive effect on total expenditures per capita, but these same incomes are associated with higher levels of local per capita expenditures. Since state (and federal) aid intervene between total and local expenditures, it is logical to conclude that local contributions to expenditures are determined on the basis of local ability, but that state aid acts to reduce the impact of variations in income on total expenditures. Here is an illustration of equalization at work on a nationwide basis. A major mechanism of this equalization process is indicated by the strong effect of state-wide personal income on total expenditures in contrast to the far smaller effect of this variable on local expenditures.

In contrast to the effects of local income, the proportion of children in the population and the proportion of pupils enrolled in secondary schools, two factors that raise costs, have higher net regression co-efficients for total per capita expenditures than for local expenditures. Again equalization is in operation because local communities do not bear the major portion of the burden of unusual educational needs. At the same time, educational services are not slighted since total per capita outlays are maintained, probably because of state and federal aid. Similar comparisons for other variables reveal whether the effect of grants-in-aid increase or diminish the relationship between expenditures and specific local or statewide variables.

Examples from the analysis of per pupil expenditure serve further to demonstrate this interpretation of differences in coefficients for total and local expenditures. The regression coefficients for total and local per pupil expenditures indicate that larger expenditures stemming from higher salaries for beginning teachers are borne by the state and not by the local community. In contrast, local school systems that have higher proportions of pupils in secondary grades and in private schools and high local incomes contribute more heavily to local than they do to total expenditures. Here the effect of state aid is to equalize total outlays despite local relationships. While such equalization is desirable for income and wealth, its effect is less appropriate for per cent in secondary grades. If more money is raised locally to finance the incremental costs of secondary education, state aid should not have the offsetting effect of equalizing total expenditures regardless of the proportion of pupils in secondary grades. Whether auxiliary health and counseling services should be subject to equalization is a less clear-cut matter. The estimated regression equations show that, for the most part, local outlays are the major source of expenditures for such services, although state and federal aid also serve to increase expenditures associated with this factor.

Demand, Supply, and Administrative Factors

Presentation of results in terms of contrasts among total local, per pupil, and per capita expenditures fails to stress the specific variables that reflect demand and supply elements and the hypotheses that underlie the structure of the estimating equations. This section discusses these aspects of the over-all analysis.

Demand. With regard to ability to pay, a major finding is that state personal income per capita has a positive effect on total per capita expenditures in contrast to its strong negative effect on local per pupil expenditures. While median family income is not important in any of the four equations, the proportion of families with incomes of $10,000 or more is positively associated with expenditures in all equations and an additional per cent in this category raises per pupil expenditures by $2.74. These results are evidence that communities dominated by middle-income families do not spend more than required to provide state-mandated or typical levels of education, and that only when there is a high concentration of families at the upper end of the income scale do communities spend more from their own resources for local schools. However, it is difficult to interpret the relationship between median family income and the proportion of incomes over $10,000. These two measures are intercorrelated and income effects may be reflected in either one or the other, or in some complex interaction between the two.

As for other factors on the demand side, there is no indication that when these factors are taken into account more is spent for education in communities in which more highly educated adults reside. Greater nonpublic school enrollments are accompanied by lower per capita expenditures on public schools, but no less is spent per pupil, and local per pupil expenditures tend to be higher. The reduced number of pupils that a local school system must provide for apparently creates a higher local capacity to finance expenditures. As hypothesized, a greater proportion of children in the population is associated with higher per capita expenditures that reflect the greater quantity of services provided. However, despite the burden of relatively more pupils, total per pupil outlays in areas with relatively large school populations are not reduced. The effect of a high proportion of families who have been in the community for less than five years is not great, but it is negative in all four equations. Finally, while simple correlations between the proportion of non-whites in the population and the four measures of expenditures are negative, all of the multiple correlations are positive. Perhaps higher costs of dual school systems and their location in states with low per capita incomes explain these differences between simple and partial correlations.

Supply. The dominance of auxiliary services in explaining per pupil expenditures has already been mentioned. The high partial correlations of this variable with per pupil expenditures are not solely a reflection of the extra spending which the provision of these auxiliary services requires. Rather, it is likely that school systems which provide extensive health and counseling services also provide an unusual quantity or quality of other auxiliary services and a high quality of regular school services as well. Further, the provision of such services is not strongly associated with levels of local income, education, or other characteristics of the community included as independent variables in this study of expenditures. The matrix of simple correlations among variables, however, reveals that auxiliary services have about the same relationship to expenditures as do each of the three measures of income, and also are correlated positively with the salaries of beginning teachers. Thus, the analysis of per pupil expenditures has not succeeded, as we hoped, in explaining quality of educational services by indirect measures of local ability to pay and preferences for education. Instead, a measure of auxiliary services appears to have acted as a proxy for cost and demand components of both the quality of education and the quantity of other auxiliary services.

The systematically positive effect of a greater proportion of pupils in secondary grades is further support of an effect well-demonstrated in previous studies. A less statistically significant and not previously demonstrated result is the verification of the hypothesized negative effect of higher amounts of school capital per pupil. The small importance of this variable in accounting for variations in school spending, however, makes this finding more a source of theoretical satisfaction than an explanation of educational spending. Density, which was expected to be inversely related to the need for transportation services, has the proper sign only in the regression for per pupil expenditures, and its effect is small. Average daily attendance, introduced to test for the presence of the ever elusive economies of scale in the operation of public facilities, fails to reveal any such tendencies.

Salaries of beginning teachers, it will be recalled, play a dual role in the analysis. On the demand side, salaries, as an indicator of the price of educational services, are expected to have a negative effect on school spending. As a measure of cost, however, higher salaries, like a higher proportion of pupils in secondary grades, require increased outlays. Coefficients for salary are positive in all four equations, and there are especially high partial correlation and beta coefficients in the equation for total per capita expenditures. The regression coefficients for teachers' salaries indicate that the higher levels of total expenditures, found in school systems where teachers salaries are greater, are not accompanied by proportionately larger local outlays; they come instead largely out of state payments to local schools. State patterns, however, are not uniform with respect to their influence on teachers' salaries (see below).

Administration and Organization. Among all relationships between institutional arrangements and spending for local public schools, the effect of fiscal dependence or independence is debated more than any other. The findings of this study indicate that fiscally dependent school systems tend to spend less in all four expenditure categories, and that total spending is influenced more by this organizational arrangement than is local spending. However, since fiscally dependent school districts are predominately located in larger cities, the relationship measured here may simply reflect the general complex of expenditure influences that tend to hold down large city school expenditures. The higher negative coefficients for total than for local expenditures thus reflect the differential impacts of state and federal aid on larger cities.

The correlation of .66 between state property per capita and statewide income serves to reduce the impact of property in the explanation of expenditures. The low coefficients for property indicate that, despite the reliance on property taxation for 53 per cent of total revenues for local school spending in 1960, states with relatively low property values utilize other taxes to tap their economic resources and those with relatively high values do not spend more as a consequence. Where the proportion (not the amounts) of revenues for local schools collected from state sources is large, total expenditures per capita are higher, but total expenditures per pupil remain the same and local expenditures are less. An explanation of these results is that in states where the proportion of children is high, and where the state participates in the collection of revenues for public schools to a greater extent,[6] spending per capita is higher as a result of the expenditure of the state collected revenues. Per pupil outlays are unaffected, however, because the increased spending is spread over more pupils.

Alternative formulas for state aid have produced almost as much

---

[6] There is a correlation of .64 between these variables (see Table A.1).

controversy as the issue of fiscal dependence or independence. A major problem of equalization formulas is that they are thought to reduce local initiative. This study does find that local per pupil expenditures are lower in school systems located in states that rely more heavily on equalization grants, although local per capita expenditures are unaffected. The estimated reduction of 32 cents in local per pupil spending for each additional per cent of equalization grants as a proportion of total state grants, however, may be an acceptable price for the more equitable burden achieved through equalization. With regard to specific versus general-purpose grants, the analysis indicates that higher per pupil outlays take place in those states that make more extensive use of general-purpose grants.

Income Elasticity. The focus of this study is not on the estimation of the income elasticity of educational expenditures. This measure of the responsiveness of expenditures to a 1 per cent increase in income is so frequently used, however, that no empirical study of the determinants of expenditures is complete without an estimate of it. Since the income variables of this study are in natural units rather than in proportions (logarithms) it is possible to estimate elasticity only around the mean. Further, account must be taken of the effect of each of the three separate income variables included in the regression equations. The procedure used under these circumstances is to determine the size of a 1 per cent increase in the mean value of each income variable, and multiply it by the appropriate net-regression coefficient. The change in the dependent variable is determined by summing the three products; elasticity at the mean is equal to the changed value of the dependent variable expressed as a per cent of its mean value.

Table 5 shows that income elasticity is greater for per capita than for per pupil expenditures. The major source of responsiveness of total expenditures to higher income levels is through state per capita income, while what little responsiveness there is in local expenditures comes from increases in local incomes. Again this pattern of reaction can be attributed to arrangements such that as state income rises state aid payments grow and lead to an increase in total expenditures for local schools. But the receipt of larger amounts of state aid necessitates less of a local response to the higher levels of family income that generally accompany the rise in state personal income per capita.

The income elasticities are quite irregular, but all exhibit a characteristically low magnitude. Failure to find a considerably greater than proportionate responsiveness of educational outlays to an increase in personal or family income should not be taken as an indication that education as an item of consumption is a "normal" rather than a

TABLE 5
INCOME ELASTICITIES OF CURRENT EXPENDITURES
FOR LOCAL PUBLIC SCHOOLS*

Dep. Var.	All measures of income†	Measures of local income only‡	State personal income per capita only
	Income Elasticity		
TE/C	1.21	.06	1.15
LE/C	.71	.37	.34
TE/P	.23	.00	.23
LE/P	-.56	.26	-.82

* Estimated around the mean.
† 1) Median family income; 2) Proportion of families with incomes of $10,000 or more; 3) State personal income per capita.
‡ 1) Median family income; 2) Proportion of families with incomes of $10,000 or more.

"luxury" good. Educational expenditures are comprised of two parts: one is consumption for the purpose of yielding immediate or future satisfactions, and the other is investment for the purpose of yielding future monetary income. Conceptually, the amount of education for consumption depends upon preferences, prices, and income, and intuitively is expected to rise more than proportionately to increases in income. The amount of education as an investment depends on the cost of education, in terms both of monetary outlays and earnings foregone, the monetary returns attributable to higher levels of education, and returns from other uses of money and resources; present levels of personal or family income and individual preferences for education as a consumption good are largely irrelevant here. Thus, the increase in outlays for education in response to or in association with differences in income must be divided into its consumption and investment components and the proportionate change in the consumption component alone must be known before income elasticity can be treated as an indication of preferences for education as a consumption good.

STATE-BY-STATE ANALYSIS

Objectives and Classifications of States

The state-by-state correlations and regressions make it possible to examine from a different perspective the findings of the over-all analysis and the generalizations derived there. In this section there are simple and partial correlation and net regression coefficients for each of the four independent variables for 21 of the 23 states in the sample.

The five statewide independent variables, of course, are omitted from the individual state analyses. The lower number of school systems in individual states than in the combined analysis required further elimination of independent variables. Therefore, such variables as median years of education and per cent moved into district in last five years, singularly unimportant in the explanation of variance in the over-all equations, were removed. Where considerations of degrees of freedom necessitated still further reduction in the number of independent variables, judgment, the results of the over-all analysis, and consideration of the nature of state aid arrangements were used to retain those variables that appeared to be of greatest interest in terms of the hypotheses presented in Chapter IV.

One important decision about the elimination of independent variables warrants special mention. The effects in the over-all analysis of the two local income variables, median family income and per cent of families with incomes of $10,000 or more, gave rise to the possibility that the correlation between high median family income and a large proportion of families in the $10,000 and over income class concealed the true effect of median family income. To give this variable a chance to demonstrate its full potential in explaining the variability of local school spending, and to reduce the number of independent variables in the individual state regressions, the proportion of families with incomes of $10,000 or over is omitted from all of the state-by-state equations.

A rough classification of states emerges from the elimination and retention of specific independent variables. Those states in the sample in which the determination of state aid to local school systems is based on equalized property values are in the north, have high per capita incomes, large nonpublic school populations, and, with the exception of Wisconsin, are predominantly urbanized industrial areas. These will be called Group I. In Group II are southern states with low per capita incomes, dual educational systems, and relatively high proportions of state revenue for local schools. Group III is a residual group which contains mainly industrial states with medium to high per capita incomes. While this classification groups states in accordance with the set of independent variables included in their analysis, it does not succeed, as subsequent sections in this chapter show, in providing uniform patterns of results.

State-by-State Simple Correlations

A brief discussion of simple correlations for each of the 23 states precedes the presentation of the partial correlations and regressions for the three groups of states.

The simple correlations for individual states shown in Tables 6 to 9 indicate whether the over-all simple correlations of Table 4 are averages of rather different individual relationships or are composites of similar trends. Although Tables 6 to 9 do not contain coefficients for all variables for all states, it is possible to make many comparisons among states and between the coefficients for various states and the over-all coefficients.

Among states there is no regular pattern of positive or negative correlation between total per capita expenditures and median family income, per cent non-white, teachers' salaries, and auxiliary services. In contrast, correlation coefficients for the values of property per capita and the per cent of children in the population and of pupils in secondary grades are consistently positive, and those for per cent in private schools and for average daily attendance persistently negative. Simple correlations of income and teachers' salaries with local per capita expenditures are less variable than with total, and are generally positive. The correlation coefficients between per cent of children and local per capita expenditures vary more, however, since over half are negative.

State-by-state simple correlations of the independent variables with per pupil expenditures appear to be more regular than those for per capita expenditures. Coefficients for median family income are generally positive and for auxiliary services there is only one state with a negative correlation. The proportion of non-whites, of pupils in secondary grades, and the number in average daily attendance differ more from state to state in their correlation with per pupil expenditures than any other of the independent variables.

The pattern found in the over-all analysis of higher simple correlations for local than for total expenditures extends to the state-by-state correlations for median family income, per capita property valuation, and teachers' salaries, but is not present in simple correlations for the other independent variables.

Group I: States with Equalized Property Valuations

Equalized property values per pupil are used in certain states directly to determine local contributions to public schools and inversely to determine state grants-in-aid. Reliance on this measure of ability to pay indicates that equalization of expenditures among local school systems is a dominant objective of state educational policy. Effective equalization should produce a pattern in which those characteristics that raise educational cost have higher partial correlation and net regression coefficients for total expenditures, while those that reflect ability to pay have higher coefficients for local expenditures.

TABLE 6

SIMPLE CORRELATIONS OF INDEPENDENT VARIABLES AND TOTAL
CURRENT EXPENDITURES, PER CAPITA BY STATES*

STATE	Y	PROP	DS	CHILD	PRIV	NON-W
				INDEPENDENT	- - - - - - -	
Alabama	−.37	—	—	.35	—	.36
California	−.25	—	—	.38	—	—
Connecticut	.69	—	—	.46	−.43	—
Delaware	.42	—	—	.52	—	—
Georgia	−.43	—	—	.42	—	.42
Illinois	—	.34	—	.30	−.01	−.30
Indiana	.28	—	—	.42	—	—
Louisiana	−.66	—	—	.08	—	.25
Maryland	−.17	—	—	.35	—	—
Massachusetts	.32	—	—	.20	−.31	—
Michigan	—	.35	—	.08	−.16	−.06
Mississippi	−.12	—	—	.08	—	.08
Missouri	−.16	—	—	.18	—	−.11
New Jersey	—	.17	—	.06	−.37	−.19
New York	−.06	.46	.41	.17	−.48	—
No. Carolina	−.28	—	—	.23	—	.32
Ohio	.09	—	.33	−.09	—	—
Pennsylvania	—	−.04	—	.31	—	—
Rhode Island	—	.41	—	.43	—	—
So. Carolina	−.29	—	—	.21	—	.21
Tennessee	.05	—	—	.15	—	−.06
Texas	.02	—	.79	.22	—	.12
Wisconsin	—	.92	.01	.18	—	—

			VARIABLES			
SAL	DEN	ADA	SEC	CAP	AUX	DEP
.00	——	-.01	.34	——	-.07	——
.20	——	-.22	.31	——	.16	——
-.21	——	-.20	.16	——	-.05	——
-.23	——	——	.02	——	——	——
.17	——	-.04	.29	——	-.20	——
-.45	——	-.44	.34	——	.15	——
.20	——	-.14	.12	——	.30	——
-.03	-.07	——	.09	——	.02	——
-.10	——	.13	-.07	——	-.06	——
-.12	——	-.13	.19	——	-.19	——
.43	——	——	.40	——	.32	——
.11	——	-.23	.18	——	-.05	——
-.08	——	-.12	.15	——	-.29	——
-.21	-.07	-.14	.31	.11	.08	——
.12	——	——	.09	——	-.18	.46
.24	——	——	.21	——	.28	——
-.09	——	-.15	.04	——	-.29	——
.10	——	-.02	.00	——	.33	——
.18	-.22	——	-.21	-.12	.15	——
.16	-.03	——	.01	.00	.16	——

* See Table 2 for an explanation of abbreviations and a description of variables.

TABLE 7
SIMPLE CORRELATIONS OF INDEPENDENT VARIABLES AND LOCAL CURRENT EXPENDITURES, PER CAPITA BY STATES*

STATE	Y	PROP	DS	CHILD	PRIV	NON-W
Alabama	−.19	—	—	.03	—	.12
California	−.60	—	—	−.12	—	—
Connecticut	.75	—	—	.32	−.28	—
Delaware	−.10	—	—	.23	—	—
Georgia	.40	—	—	−.43	—	−.13
Illinois	—	.42	—	.22	.05	—
Indiana	.38	—	—	.40	—	—
Louisiana	−.06	—	—	−.03	—	.07
Maryland	.37	—	—	−.09	—	—
Massachusetts	.40	—	—	.09	−.22	—
Michigan	—	.69	—	−.03	−.10	.11
Mississippi	.22	—	—	−.04	—	.15
Missouri	.41	—	—	.09	—	−.25
New Jersey	—	.18	—	−.22	−.18	−.14
New York	.36	.54	.36	−.09	.08	—
No. Carolina	.05	—	—	−.08	—	.21
Ohio	.40	—	.16	−.40	—	—
Pennsylvania	—	.75	—	−.20	—	—
Rhode Island	—	.33	—	.01	—	—
So. Carolina	.18	—	—	−.19	—	−.20
Tennessee	.67	—	—	−.33	—	.36
Texas	.10	—	.86	.18	—	.06
Wisconsin	—	.92	−.02	.08	—	—

			VARIABLES			
SAL	DEN	ADA	SEC	CAP	AUX	DEP
-.08	——	-.08	.04	——	.08	——
.22	——	-.05	.28	——	.13	——
.29	——	.38	.27	——	-.06	——
-.16	——	——	-.07	——	——	——
.19	——	-.04	.15	——	-.18	——
-.30	——	-.02	-.03	——	.38	——
.19	——	-.07	.19	——	.26	——
.21	.12	——	.04	——	.13	——
.54	——	.18	.05	——	-.06	——
.22	——	.05	.54	——	.30	——
.37	——	——	.56	——	.38	——
.24	——	-.04	.13	——	.10	——
.12	——	.23	.23	——	——	——
.21	.09	.27	.08	.02	.04	——
.09	——	——	-.10	——	.09	-.36
.42	——	——	.45	——	.20	——
.06	——	.02	.08	——	.18	——
.72	——	.48	.18	——	.32	——
.23	-.12	——	-.17	-.07	.18	——
.08	.11	——	.08	.06	.08	——

* See Table 2 for an explanation of abbreviations and a description of variables.

TABLE 8

SIMPLE CORRELATIONS OF INDEPENDENT VARIABLES AND TOTAL
CURRENT EXPENDITURES, PER PUPIL BY STATES*

STATE	INDEPENDENT - - - - - - -					
	Y	PROP	DS	CHILD	PRIV	NON-W
Alabama	-.15	—	—	.11	—	.08
California	.00	—	—	-.19	—	—
Connecticut	.13	—	—	.05	-.11	—
Delaware	.62	—	—	—	—	—
Georgia	-.26	—	—	.20	—	.41
Illinois	—	-.19	—	-.05	.33	.16
Indiana	.03	—	—	.07	—	—
Louisiana	-.45	—	—	-.32	—	.13
Maryland	.32	—	—	—	—	—
Massachusetts	.25	—	—	-.11	.22	—
Michigan	—	.06	—	-.03	.15	-.07
Mississippi	.45	—	—	-.40	—	-.40
Missouri	.43	—	.38	.04	—	.04
New Jersey	—	.14	—	-.38	.23	-.04
New York	.32	.46	.16	-.06	-.04	.08
No. Carolina	.33	—	—	-.32	—	.10
Ohio	.08	—	-.05	-.20	—	—
Pennsylvania	—	.58	—	-.27	—	—
Rhode Island	—	.19	—	-.28	—	—
So. Carolina	.39	—	—	-.37	—	-.35
Tennessee	.59	—	—	-.39	—	.25
Texas	.09	—	.73	.04	—	.05
Wisconsin	—	.26	.10	-.05	—	—

- - - - - - - VARIABLES							
SAL	DEN	ADA	SEC	CAP	AUX	DEP	MIGR
.02	—	.03	-.07	—	.41	—	—
.17	.01	.12	.70	.09	.30	—	-.15
.16	—	-.11	.01	—	.65	—	—
—	—	—	.44	—	—	—	—
-.16	—	-.14	-.10	—	.34	—	—
.32	—	-.02	.81	—	.75	—	—
.19	—	.20	.39	—	.10	—	—
-.38	—	-.15	.39	—	.27	—	—
—	—	—	-.32	—	—	—	—
.06	—	.00	.65	—	.47	—	—
.20	.25	—	.01	—	.99	—	—
.23	—	.16	.22	—	.04	—	—
.23	.10	—	—	—	.57	—	—
.37	—	.26	.45	—	.39	—	—
.28	—	-.06	.26	—	.52	—	—
.42	—	.22	.19	—	—	—	—
.02	.17	.07	.55	.83	.50	—	—
.36	—	—	.41	—	.04	-.12	—
.21	—	—	-.05	—	-.09	—	—
.17	—	.11	.29	—	—	—	—
.60	—	.29	.23	—	.39	—	—
.20	.17	—	-.05	-.06	.16	—	—
.37	.35	—	.26	.65	.51	—	—

* See Table 2 for an explanation of abbreviations and a description of variables.

TABLE 9

SIMPLE CORRELATIONS OF INDEPENDENT VARIABLES AND LOCAL
CURRENT EXPENDITURES, PER PUPIL BY STATES*

STATE	Y	PROP	DS	CHILD	PRIV	NON-W
Alabama	–.19	——	——	.03	——	.12
California	.09	——	——	–.05	——	——
Connecticut	.18	——	——	.02	–.09	——
Delaware	–.09	——	——	——	——	——
Georgia	.41	——	——	–.42	——	–.09
Illinois	——	–.21	——	–.03	.39	.13
Indiana	.16	——	——	.04	——	——
Louisiana	.02	——	——	–.07	——	.05
Maryland	.41	——	——	——	——	——
Massachusetts	.32	——	——	–.18	——	——
Michigan	——	.13	——	–.05	.16	–.03
Mississippi	.35	——	——	–.17	——	.01
Missouri	.64	——	.56	–.03	——	–.11
New Jersey	——	.16	——	.35	.31	–.15
New York	.44	.43	.18	–.25	.31	.30
No. Carolina	.15	——	——	–.18	——	.15
Ohio	.47	——	.01	–.51	——	——
Pennsylvania	——	.67	——	–.37	——	——
Rhode Island	——	.18	——	–.41	——	——
So. Carolina	.36	——	——	–.33	——	–.33
Tennessee	.65	——	——	–.40	——	.42
Texas	.16	——	.77	.11	——	.01
Wisconsin	——	.20	.09	–.13	——	——

			VARIABLES			
SAL	DEN	ADA	SEC	CAP	AUX	DEP
-.08	—	-.08	.04	—	.08	—
.04	.10	.13	.24	—	.23	—
.19	—	-.03	.11	—	.65	—
—	—	—	-.24	—	—	—
.28	—	.38	.20	—	.02	—
.38	—	-.03	.78	—	.75	—
.10	—	.14	.16	—	.19	—
-.24	—	.08	-.04	—	.37	—
—	—	—	-.18	—	—	—
.07	—	.07	.68	—	.40	—
.25	.29	—	.00	—	.98	—
.59	—	.23	.00	—	-.05	—
.38	—	.19	—	—	.62	—
.35	—	.29	.48	—	.43	—
.27	—	.08	.19	—	.18	—
.19	—	.30	—	—	—	—
.42	.48	.26	.01	.18	.16	—
.30	—	—	.17	—	.13	-.36
.44	—	—	.53	—	-.15	—
.19	—	.11	.04	—	—	—
.68	—	.50	.08	—	.27	—
.23	-.07	—	-.08	-.06	.14	—
.15	.41	—	.14	.32	.32	—

* See Table 2 for an explanation of abbreviations and a description of variables.

Since equalization refers to services provided to pupils, differences should be more pronounced for per pupil than for per capita spending.

Property Value Per Capita. Tables 10 and 11 show that, for all states except New Jersey and Illinois, higher equalized property values per capita are associated with larger expenditures and have greater effect on local than on total outlays. The most substantial equalization of the effect of ability to pay is in Pennsylvania and Michigan where the partial correlations for property value per capita are far higher for local than for total expenditures. On the other hand, in Rhode Island and Wisconsin total expenditures have a stronger positive relation with property values than do local expenditures. Here the effect of state aid, when other factors are taken into account, is to aggravate inequalities in total expenditures in accordance with property valuation per capita. In the determination of both per pupil and per capita expenditures in New Jersey and of per pupil expenditures in Illinois, property values have little effect on either total or local expenditures.

Other Demand Factors. Total per capita outlays are higher where the proportion of children is larger, but local per capita outlays are not affected. Unlike the results of the over-all analysis, its effect in most of these states is to reduce total per pupil outlays and to lower local per pupil spending even more. Thus, equalization tends to spread the burden of a relatively larger number of children to be educated among school districts in the state, but without fully offsetting the tendency toward lower expenditures per pupil in such areas.

The effect of a higher proportion of children in nonpublic schools is similar here to its effect in the over-all analysis. Total expenditures per capita are generally lower as a reflection of a smaller proportion of children in public schools and local per pupil expenditures are a bit higher. The coefficients for Illinois, however, are the reverse of those for the other states.

In all three northern states in which the proportion of non-white appears as an independent variable, it is negatively related to both total and local per capita expenditures. Only in New Jersey, however, does the negative influence extend to per pupil outlays. These results, unlike those for this variable in the over-all analysis, conform to some extent to the relationship hypothesized in Chapter IV.

Cost Factors. The proportion of pupils in secondary grades, although generally associated positively with expenditures, especially per pupil expenditures, does not appear to be subject to equalization. The net regression coefficients and partial correlation coefficients for total and local per pupil spending indicate that local schools in these states bear a major share of the increased costs of secondary education and that in Illinois, New Jersey, and New York the net effect of state aid tends to reduce spending in school systems with greater proportions of secondary pupils.[7]

Higher teachers' salaries are associated with lower per capita spending in three of these seven states. Only in Michigan is its effect also negative for per pupil outlays. Where increased spending is associated with higher levels of teachers' salaries, the net regression coefficient for local expenditures is generally greater than that for total expenditures, indicating that the costs of higher teachers' salaries, on the whole, are not equalized among school systems. The negative coefficients for Michigan and Illinois are an indication that teachers' salaries do have an effect through the demand side, and that in these two states, when account is taken of other variables, less is spent in communities where teachers' salaries are higher. It should be noted that for Michigan, where the partial correlation coefficient for teachers' salaries is negative in all four equations, the simple correlation coefficient is positive in three out of the four.

Auxiliary Services. The extent of auxiliary services is an especially significant factor in per pupil expenditures among these states even as it is in the over-all analysis. In Michigan the partial correlation coefficient for this variable explains virtually all of the variation in per pupil expenditures. In this state, apparently, the only systematic variations from average per pupil expenditures are for auxiliary health and counseling services or cost and demand factors highly correlated with these services. Except for Rhode Island, greater provision of auxiliary services is associated more regularly and has a larger effect on local than on total expenditures.

Other Variables. Analysis of those states with a relatively large number of observations permits the inclusion of a few additional independent variables. Debt service per capita, which appears in the regressions for Wisconsin and New York, is associated with higher outlays in all expenditure categories. This finding does not conform to the hypothesis that debt service is an offset to ability to pay for current outlays, but is consistent with the alternative view that large school indebtedness indicates a favorable attitude toward education. The effect of density in the two states in which it appears is at vari-

---

[7] Evidence for the direction of the net effect of state aid is that the net regression coefficients for proportion in secondary grades for each of these three states are higher for local per pupil expenditures than for total per pupil expenditures. The lower effect of this independent variable on total than on local expenditures is attributable to the influence of state and perhaps federal aid.

TABLE 10
PARTIAL CORRELATION COEFFICIENTS FOR STATES WITH EQUALIZED PROPERTY VALUATIONS (GROUP I)*

DEP. VAR.	STATE	PROP	DS	CHILD	PRIV	NON-W	SAL
					INDEPENDENT		
TE / C	Illinois	.21	—	.28	.30	-.13	-.33
	Michigan	.40‡	—	.00	-.13	-.13	-.19
	New Jersey	-.10	—	-.02	-.40‡	-.34‡	.35‡
	New York	.47	.41‡	.19	-.48‡	—	-.01
	Pennsylvania	.14	—	.29	—	—	.20
	Rhode Island	.57‡	—	.60‡	—	—	.29
	Wisconsin	.94‡	.21	.06	—	—	.28‡
LE / C	Illinois	.31‡	—	.16	.26	-.11	-.25
	Michigan	.68‡	—	-.12	-.12	-.13	-.13
	New Jersey	-.07	—	-.08	-.11	-.33‡	.26
	New York	.49‡	.25	-.06	.13	—	.04
	Pennsylvania	.74‡	—	.08	—	—	.19
	Rhode Island	.44‡	—	.09	—	—	.36
	Wisconsin	.92‡	.19	-.02	—	—	.07
TE / P	Illinois	-.17	—	-.46‡	-.11	.17	.21
	Michigan	.11	—	.14	.02	.01	-.20
	New Jersey	-.02	—	-.43‡	.18	-.11	.40‡
	New York	.42‡	.01	-.14	-.08	—	.17
	Pennsylvania	.54‡	—	-.07	—	—	.35‡
	Rhode Island	.30	—	-.30	—	—	.29
	Wisconsin	.15	.22	.02	—	—	.17
LE / P	Illinois	-.19	—	-.08	-.04	.04	.28‡
	Michigan	.39‡	—	-.05	.05	.10	-.08
	New Jersey	-.01	—	-.43‡	.22	-.25	.37‡
	New York	.40‡	.09	-.24	.31‡	—	.14
	Pennsylvania	.63‡	—	-.20	—	—	.27
	Rhode Island	.16	—	-.28	—	—	.09
	Wisconsin	.13	.20	-.04	—	—	.02

DEN	ADA	SEC	CAP	AUX	DEP	R†	N
		VARIABLES					
—	—	-.05	—	—	—	.56	29
.05	—	-.07	—	.03	—	.45	55
—	—	.30	—	.37‡	—	.71	39
—	-.14	.14	—	-.31‡	—	.76	53
—	—	.20	—	-.10	.36	.56	29
—	—	.15	—	.65‡	—	.82	18
-.23	—	.00	-.20	-.01	—	.94	57
—	—	-.03	—	—	—	.53	29
.12	—	-.06	—	.11	—	.71	55
—	—	.49‡	—	.43‡	—	.73	39
—	-.07	.13	—	-.01	—	.61	52
—	—	-.12	—	.16	-.17	.79	28
—	—	.11	—	.39	—	.68	18
.14	—	.20	-.20	.09	—	.93	57
—	-.11	.61‡	—	.45‡	—	.87	61
.08	—	-.07	—	.99‡	—	.99	62
—	-.05	.29	—	.36‡	—	.71	57
—	-.02	.47‡	—	.47‡	—	.68	66
—	—	.42‡	—	-.04	-.16	.73	37
—	—	-.35	—	.08	—	.49	24
.21	—	.31‡	.41‡	.40‡	—	.77	63
—	-.12	.56‡	—	.41‡	—	.86	69
.15	—	-.19	—	.98‡	—	.99	62
—	.02	.33‡	—	.43‡	—	.56	56
—	-.01	.49‡	—	.20	—	.63	65
—	—	.20	—	.13	-.31	.77	36
—	—	.31	—	-.06	—	.61	24
.36‡	—	.23	-.01	.24	—	.75	63

* See Table 2 for an explanation of abbreviations and a description of variables.
† Multiple correlation coefficients are uncorrected for degrees of freedom.
‡ Significant at .95 level of probability under assumptions of simple random sampling, homogeneous variances, and other conditions for the application of conventional confidence intervals.

TABLE 11
NET REGRESSION COEFFICIENTS FOR STATES WITH
EQUALIZED PROPERTY VALUATIONS (GROUP I)*

DEP. VAR.	STATE	CONSTANT	PROP	DS	CHILD	PRIV
				INDEPENDENT - - - - - - -		
TE / C	Illinois	179.83	.10	——	2.71	1.36
	Michigan	272.49	1.45†	——	.00	-.70
	New Jersey	-73.73	-.03	——	-.08	-.72†
	New York	25.11	.50	.48†	1.30	-1.59†
	Pennsylvania	-78.45	.15	——	1.30	——
	Rhode Island	-137.28	.23†	——	2.15†	——
	Wisconsin	-74.47	1.33†	.55	.30	——
LE / C	Illinois	121.22	.12†	——	1.17	.90
	Michigan	82.60	1.10†	——	-.55	-.23
	New Jersey	-95.60	-.02	——	-.40	-.22
	New York	-25.13	.63†	.34	-.45	.48
	Pennsylvania	-33.11	.81†	——	.21	——
	Rhode Island	-181.32	.27†	——	.42	——
	Wisconsin	-22.13	.91†	.36	-.08	——
TE / P	Illinois	58.53	-.04	——	-.85†	-.78
	Michigan	527.78	1.13	——	5.23	.28
	New Jersey	-52.93	-.03	——	-7.70†	1.19
	New York	273.74	1.28†	.17	-2.44	-.63
	Pennsylvania	-2.30	2.18†	——	-.83	——
	Rhode Island	259.71	.70	——	-5.66	——
	Wisconsin	135.22	.16	1.10	.25	——
LE / P	Illinois	-241.06	-.05	——	-1.93	-.38
	Michigan	140.52	2.76†	——	-.12	.55
	New Jersey	-357.63	-.02	——	-11.57†	2.27
	New York	-120.70	2.35†	.56	-8.24	5.23†
	Pennsylvania	-249.99	4.86†	——	-4.26	——
	Rhode Island	322.73	.44	——	-7.16	——
	Wisconsin	112.12	.36	2.48	-.94	——

			VARIABLES				
NON-W	SAL	DEN	ADA	SEC	CAP	AUX	DEP
-.78	-4.80	—	—	-.22	—	—	—
-1.06	-4.35	.10	—	-.66	—	.29	—
-.87†	3.23†	—	—	.53	—	4.61†	—
—	-.12	—	.00	1.42	—	-4.78†	—
—	1.72	—	—	.53	—	-.84	12.40
—	2.02	—	—	.21	—	6.23†	—
—	1.87†	-.20	—	.01	-.01	-.29	—
-.52	-2.76	—	—	-.09	—	—	—
-.38	-1.04	.08	—	-.20	—	.39	—
-.98†	2.75	—	—	1.08†	—	6.48†	—
—	.45	—	.00	.68	—	-.21	—
—	1.05	—	—	-.24	—	.91	-3.36
—	4.15	—	—	+.24	—	4.97	—
—	.37	.09	—	.41	-.06	1.53	—
2.29	6.67	—	-.02	1.91†	—	22.39†	—
2.38	-13.53	.45	—	-.84	—	181.85†	—
-.91	15.13†	—	-.08	.87	—	16.68†	—
—	4.37	—	.00	1.08†	—	22.69†	—
—	7.96†	—	—	.95†	—	-.90	-13.94
—	7.96	—	—	-1.30	—	2.72	—
—	2.15	.38	—	.98†	.33†	18.44†	—
.69	11.54†	—	-.02	2.23†	—	26.40†	—
1.63	-3.56	.56	—	-1.49	—	111.06†	—
-3.30	20.94†	—	.03	1.52†	—	31.29†	—
—	7.10	—	.00	2.01†	—	16.80	—
—	10.18	—	—	.70	—	5.02	-50.05
—	3.15	—	—	1.54	—	-2.60	—
—	.47	1.70†	—	1.72	-.01	25.54	—

* See Table 2 for an explanation of abbreviations and a description of variables.
† Significant at .95 level of probability under assumptions of simple random sampling, homogeneous variances, and other conditions for the application of conventional confidence intervals.

ance with the hypothesis that lower density is associated with higher expenditures through its effects on transportation costs. This hypothesis may still be correct, however. Perhaps the failure to confirm it is a consequence of not taking account of other factors positively correlated with both density and expenditures.

Group II: Southern States

Virtually the same seven independent variables were used in the analysis of each of seven southern states that maintain *de jure* segregation in elementary and secondary schools.[8] Elements that reflect demand are median family income and proportion of children and of non-whites in the population. Supply factors considered for these states include auxiliary services, average daily attendance, per cent in secondary grades, and salaries of beginning teachers. The results are shown in Tables 12 and 13.

Demand. Total per capita expenditures in these southern states are higher in school systems that have a greater proportion of children and lower where median family income is higher. The effect of the proportion of children on the other dependent variables is to reduce total per pupil expenditures somewhat and to lower local per pupil spending even more. The equalization apparent in these findings carries over to the influence of median family income where, in almost every cell, local expenditures are more positively influenced by higher incomes than are total expenditures. The relationship of total per capita expenditures to median family income is negative for all states except Tennessee, where this variable is positively associated with local expenditures throughout.

There is no evidence that in these states a relatively larger non-white population is associated with lower current expenditures. Where significant coefficients are found they indicate higher spending in such communities. The simple correlations also, for the most part, are positive, an indication that the negative simple correlations between the proportion of non-whites and expenditures found in the over-all analysis stems from negative relationships in the non-southern states of the sample. The contrast between the positive effect of this variable in these southern states and its negative influence in several of the northern states may possibly arise from expenditure efforts designed

---

[8] Texas, which also has *de jure* segregation, is included in the next group of states because the large number of observations obtained made possible the inclusion of several additional independent variables so that results for Texas are more comparable with those for states in the third group.

to defend a "separate-but-equal" school system. It may also be attributable to the dual education system in the South which is more costly because of the need to duplicate administrative and supervisory personnel. The issue is not so simple, however, because average daily attendance, a measure of school system size and hence of the scope for economies of scale, is included in these regressions and should thus serve to take economies of scale into account.

Supply. The proportion of pupils in secondary grades is a cost factor which, unlike its influence in the northern states, is positively associated with larger total expenditures in almost all of these southern states. Net regression coefficients for this variable for local expenditures are consistently lower than those for total expenditures and, for some states, are negative. On the whole, there is greater equalization of expenditures in school systems that have high proportions of secondary school pupils than in the northern states that use property values for equalization purposes. However, per pupil expenditures in North Carolina and Georgia run counter to this general trend.

Evidence of economies of scale is lacking among southern states as it is in the over-all analysis and in the separate regression for New York, since the number of pupils in average daily attendance has little effect on expenditures.

With the exception of South Carolina, higher levels of teachers' salaries have a negative influence on one or more categories of expenditures in all of these states. In contrast to the northern states, where expenditures in only two states were negatively affected by this variable, in the South there seems to be less of a tendency for school systems that face higher salaries, and perhaps higher costs of other inputs as well, to offset these costs by larger outlays. The size of the negative regression coefficients is almost trivial except for Louisiana and Missouri and high partial correlation coefficients are primarily found in the few states where the effect of teachers' salaries is positive.

The regression coefficients for auxiliary services among the southern states are considerably lower than those for the northern states, but the same pattern of importance in per pupil spending and insignificance for per capita expenditures again is found. As with the northern group, some states show none of the high simple and partial correlations with auxiliary services. In those states where the relationship is strong, the effect on local expenditures almost equals or exceeds the effect on total expenditures, indicating that primary support for outlays for auxiliary services comes from local rather than state sources.

TABLE 12

PARTIAL CORRELATION COEFFICIENTS FOR SOUTHERN STATES (GROUP II)*

DEP. VAR.	STATE	INDEPENDENT — — — — — —			
		Y	DS	CHILD	NON-W
TE/C	Alabama	-.09	——	.13	.21
	Georgia	-.19	——	.18	.14
	Louisiana	-.29	——	.02	.18
	Mississippi	-.11	——	-.01	-.05
	Missouri	-.29	.45‡	.05	-.18
	No. Carolina	-.10	——	.02	.20
	So. Carolina	-.20	——	.05	-.07
	Tennessee	.06	——	.25	.04
LE/C	Alabama	——	——	——	——
	Georgia	.20	——	-.43‡	.31‡
	Louisiana	.02	——	-.11	.03
	Mississippi	.05	——	-.01	.11
	Missouri	.03	.47‡	-.13	-.28
	No. Carolina	.00	——	-.20	.35‡
	So. Carolina	.00	——	-.05	-.09
	Tennessee	.31‡	——	-.10	.28
TE/P	Alabama	-.18	——	.16	.03
	Georgia	-.02	——	-.03	.29‡
	Louisiana	-.32	——	-.46‡	-.08
	Mississippi	.07	——	-.03	-.19
	Missouri	.06	.18	.01	.16
	No. Carolina	.18	——	-.31‡	.47‡
	So. Carolina	.05	——	-.13	-.08
	Tennessee	.34‡	——	-.27	.18
LE/P	Alabama	——	——	——	——
	Georgia	.24	——	-.42‡	.34‡
	Louisiana	.03	——	-.12	.02
	Mississippi	.09	——	-.03	.07
	Missouri	.26	.31	-.23	-.06
	No. Carolina	.06	——	-.25	.39‡
	So. Carolina	.10	——	-.10	-.08
	Tennessee	.30‡	——	-.23	.36‡

SAL	ADA	SEC	AUX	R†	N
		VARIABLES			
.05	.11	.35‡	.09	.54	52
-.09	.07	.16	-.16	.55	54
-.40‡	-.41‡	.49‡	-.19	.82	31
-.02	.19	-.03	-.10	.25	39
-.13	.00	——	-.09	.53	41
-.01	-.11	.26	——	.43	47
-.07	-.06	.15	——	.34	39
-.04	-.01	.09	.36‡	.42	49
.10	.18	.38‡	-.07	.67	55
-.20	-.01	-.17	.32	.46	31
.40‡	.03	-.05	-.02	.56	39
-.21	.06	——	.07	.63	41
-.03	.25	.21	——	.47	47
.09	-.05	.03	——	.23	39
.36‡	.10	.16	.31‡	.83	49
.06	.14	.00	.45‡	.48	52
-.08	.03	-.17	.30‡	.67	55
-.30	-.15	.19	.06	.72	31
.11	.08	.17	-.02	.52	39
-.22	-.01	——	.47‡	.63	41
.26	.19	.05	——	.64	47
.19	.00	.20	——	.49	39
.33‡	-.11	.43‡	.37‡	.81	55
.10	.16	.29‡	.05	.65	55
-.16	.07	-.20	.32	.46	31
.44‡	.07	-.14	-.01	.62	39
-.21	.07	——	.37‡	.75	41
-.02	.33‡	.19	——	.54	47
.22	-.02	-.09	——	.44	39
.37‡	.17	.17	.25	.84	54

* See Table 2 for an explanation of abbreviations and a description of variables.
† Multiple correlation coefficients are uncorrected for degrees of freedom.
‡ Significant at .95 level of probability under assumptions of simple random sampling, homogeneous variances, and other conditions for the application of conventional confidence intervals.

TABLE 13
NET REGRESSION COEFFICIENTS FOR SOUTHERN STATES (GROUP II)*

DEP. VAR.	STATE	CONSTANT	INDEXPENDENT — — — — — — —		
			Y	DS	CHILD
TE / C	Alabama	-7.09	-.05	——	.44
	Georgia	26.19	-.25	——	.69
	Louisiana	115.93	-.53	——	.07
	Mississippi	73.71	-.67	——	-.10
	Missouri	99.47	-.64	5.05†	.25
	No. Carolina	30.05	-.14	——	.07
	So. Carolina	58.57	-.80	——	.26
	Tennessee	-12.49	.13	——	1.35
LE / C	Alabama	——	——	——	——
	Georgia	27.59	.19	——	-1.26†
	Louisiana	89.33	.05	——	-.56
	Mississippi	-46.64	.11	——	-.02
	Missouri	99.47	.04	3.54†	-.46
	No. Carolina	30.05	.00	——	-.47
	So. Carolina	10.91	-.01	——	-.11
	Tennessee	-21.70	.26†	——	-.20
TE / P	Alabama	172.86	-.35	——	.18
	Georgia	246.58	-.06	——	-.35
	Louisiana	700.50	-1.49	——	-5.01†
	Mississippi	157.06	.40	——	-.33
	Missouri	420.68	.43	6.10	.18
	No. Carolina	186.74	.44	——	-1.72†
	So. Carolina	149.75	.24	——	-.85
	Tennessee	154.65	1.10†	——	-2.34
LE / P	Alabama	——	——	——	——
	Georgia	149.75	1.22	——	-6.78†
	Louisiana	372.58	.33	——	-2.77
	Mississippi	-177.78	.85	——	-.48
	Missouri	362.09	2.05	12.09	-4.30
	No. Carolina	48.79	.26	——	-2.69
	So. Carolina	30.40	.64	——	-8.81
	Tennessee	-44.36	1.21†	——	-2.52

* See Table 5 for an explanation of abbreviations and a description of variables.

	VARIABLES			
NON-W	SAL	ADA	SEC	AUX
.12	.08	.01	.59†	2.17
.10	−.22	.01	.19	−1.45
.24	−2.06†	−.05†	1.82†	−3.79
−.11	−.19	2.31	−.09	−4.07
−.69	−1.02	.00	⸺	−2.49
.15	−.03	−.02	.65	⸺
−.16	−.31	−.02	.54	⸺
.67	−.17	−.00	.14	3.48†
.17†	.19	.02	.33†	−.41
.06	−1.34	.00	−.79	9.14
.12	1.46†	.02	−.05	.34
−.74	−1.13	.01	⸺	1.17
.19†	−.06	.03	.39	⸺
−.10	.19	−.01	.04	⸺
.19	.75†	.00	.10	1.09†
.05	.32	.04	−.01	39.10†
.66†	−.54	.13	−.57	8.26†
−.28	−3.74	−.04	1.55	3.04
−.48	.88	.10	.50	−.91
2.09	−5.69	−.01	⸺	47.89†
.64†	1.22	.06	.21	⸺
−.23	1.07	.00	.90	⸺
.42	2.45†	−.19	.74†	5.46†
1.03†	.94	.98	1.29†	1.69
.17	−4.74	.04	−3.88	40.78
.29	6.60†	.14	−.67	−.76
−.83	−6.15	.07	⸺	38.60†
.95†	−.18	.22†	1.55	⸺
−.29	1.74	−.01	−.53	⸺
1.08†	3.64†	.04	.34	4.26

* See Table 2 for an explanation of abbreviations and a description of variables.
† Significant at .95 level of probability under assumptions of simple random sampling, homogeneous variances, and other conditions for the application of conventional confidence intervals.

Debt service has an influence in Missouri similar to that found in New York and Wisconsin. It exerts a positive effect on all categories of expenditures and has significantly high regression coefficients for all of the dependent variables save total per pupil expenditures.

Group III: Remaining States

The residual group includes states with varying numbers of observations and characteristics. Consequently the number and nature of the independent variables introduced into the analysis differs among these states, and results are even less comparable than for the other two groups. The findings are set forth in Tables 14 and 15.

Demand. Median family income has more of a positive effect on the determination of expenditures among these states than it does in the southern states. The pattern of regression and correlation coefficients for median family income indicates that state aid payments serve to equalize the effects of local ability to pay on total expenditures in all of these states except Connecticut, where its effect is neutral. Ohio in particular achieves considerable equalization since in this state there is virtually no association between income and either per pupil or per capita total expenditures, while family income is significantly positive for both categories of local expenditures. Indiana attains similar equalization effects for per pupil spending.

The response to a larger proportion of children in the population among these states follows the general pattern for the other groups: per capita outlays are higher and per pupil outlays lower. Debt service introduced into the analysis for Texas and Ohio has relatively little effect in the latter, but is responsible for almost all the variance explained for the former. In Texas the partial correlation coefficients for debt service range from .72 to .84 and the simple correlations are almost as large. Although debt service also exhibited a strong positive association with school expenditures in Wisconsin, New York, and Missouri, in none of these states were its effects so great. It would appear that in Texas this variable, like auxiliary services in many other states, is highly correlated with the provision of educational services not reflected by other variables included in the analysis.

Higher proportions of nonpublic school enrollments in Massachusetts and Connecticut are associated with lower total per capita outlays. In Connecticut per pupil spending also is lower, but in Massachusetts per pupil expenditures are higher in school systems where there are relatively more nonpublic school students. School capital, included in the equations for California, Texas, and Ohio, has the unusually high positive partial correlation of .73 with total per pupil expenditures in Ohio. For the other two states it follows the pattern found in the over-all analysis of low negative coefficients.

Supply. Average daily attendance again fails to provide substantiation for the presence of economies of scale in this group of states. California and Texas, where there are many sparsely populated school systems, show negative coefficients for density, but the effect is small. Percentage of pupils in secondary grades reveals the typical pattern. Total expenditures are influenced to a greater extent and more regularly than local. Equalization through state aid is taking place, although the regression coefficients for Massachusetts and Connecticut indicate that in these two states local communities bear the major share of the higher outlays that accompany relatively more pupils in secondary grades. Teachers' salaries on the whole are associated with higher spending among these states, but the positive effect is smaller and less regular than is found for the northern states. Only Connecticut runs counter to the group, with a negative relationship between per pupil expenditures and higher teachers' salaries.

CONCLUSIONS AND IMPLICATIONS

The results of the empirical study of factors associated with public expenditures can be evaluated from several viewpoints. A major concern of the analysis was to test an economic model of government behavior which assumed that the expenditure decisions of local school officials were based on a pattern of rational economic motives. A second interest was the investigation on a comparable basis of simple and multivariate quantitative relationships between local school expenditures and a series of characteristics of communities for a nationwide sample of school systems. A third aspect of the study distinguished the effects of the same determinants on per capita and on per pupil spending. A final element involved the estimation of the influence of state and federal grants-in-aid for education on local spending in school systems in a set of states representative of different grant arrangements. These four aspects of the empirical study are, of course, interrelated; it is the character of the model which determined the specific state and local characteristics used as independent variables. Nevertheless, it is appropriate to evaluate each aspect separately.

The Economic Model of Governmental Behavior

Although a number of the hypotheses that underlie the over-all model of governmental behavior are supported by the statistical anal-

TABLE 14

PARTIAL CORRELATION COEFFICIENTS FOR RESIDUAL STATES (GROUP III)*

DEP. VAR.	STATE	Y	DS	CHILD	PRIV	NON-W	MIGR
				INDEPENDENT	- - - - - - -		
TE / C	California	−.36	—	.45	—	—	—
	Connecticut	.59‡	—	.37‡	−.08	—	—
	Indiana	.29	—	.37‡	—	—	—
	Massachusetts	.29	—	.13	−.22	—	—
	Ohio	.09	.36‡	−.13	—	—	—
	Texas	−.04	.75‡	.17	—	.19	—
LE / C	California	−.59‡	—	.00	—	—	—
	Connecticut	.66‡	—	.22	.06	—	—
	Indiana	.35‡	—	.33‡	—	—	—
	Massachusetts	.39‡	—	.03	−.16	—	—
	Ohio	.35‡	.16	−.42‡	—	—	—
	Texas	.09	.84‡	.03	—	.02	—
TE / P	California	.13	—	−.16	—	—	−.14
	Connecticut	.09	—	.05	−.04	—	—
	Indiana	.01	—	.05	—	—	—
	Massachusetts	.37‡	—	−.24	.31‡	—	—
	Ohio	−.02	−.10	−.11	—	—	—
	Texas	.08	.72‡	−.15	—	−.04	—
LE / P	California	.11	—	.01	—	—	−.19
	Connecticut	.13	—	.04	−.04	—	—
	Indiana	.15	—	−.01	—	—	—
	Massachusetts	.48‡	—	−.38‡	.26	—	—
	Ohio	.41‡	−.04	−.52‡	—	—	—
	Texas	.17	.75‡	−.09	—	−.09	—

SAL	DEN	ADA	SEC	CAP	AUX	R†	N
						.50	15
.06	—	-.18	.38‡	—	.06	.81	52
.01	—	.07	-.35‡	—	-.29	.60	44
.10	—	.03	.03	—	.38‡	.55	45
-.20	-.01	.02	.30‡	-.11	.05	.52	72
.09	-.20	—	-.07	-.15	-.11	.82	84
						.60	15
.02	—	-.07	.26	—	.01	.78	52
.04	—	.00	.21	—	-.25	.57	44
.07	—	.06	.11	—	.33‡	.54	44
.02	.05	-.01	.12	-.15	.01	.60	72
.09	-.02	—	-.02	-.06	-.09	.86	84
.21	-.19	-.02	.67‡	.09	-.01	.74	79
-.15	—	.06	.07	—	.65‡	.67	61
.13	—	.31‡	.44‡	—	.07	.51	46
.04	—	.02	.70‡	—	.51‡	.82	51
.03	.07	.01	.27‡	.73‡	.27	.87	72
.05	-.10	—	.07	-.06	-.03	.75	85
.02	-.01	.04	.14	-.06	.15	.38	79
-.14	—	.12	.17	—	.66‡	.70	61
.04	—	.11	.18	—	.19	.34	46
.01	—	.10	.75‡	—	.46‡	.85	50
.19	.14	.04	-.08	.09	.08	.75	72
.09	.04	—	.03	-.05	-.08	.78	85

VARIABLES

* See Table 2 for an explanation of abbreviations and a description of variables.
† Multiple correlation coefficients are uncorrected for degrees of freedom.
‡ Significant at .95 level of probability under assumptions of simple random sampling, homogeneous variances, and other conditions for the application of conventional confidence intervals.

TABLE 15
REGRESSION COEFFICIENTS FOR RESIDUAL STATES (GROUP III)*

DEP. VAR.	STATE	CONSTANT	Y	DS	CHILD	PRIV
				INDEPENDENT - - - - - - -		
TE/C	California	99.86	-1.49	——	2.25	——
	Connecticut	-85.49	.90†	——	1.90†	-.11
	Indiana	-93.18	.77	——	2.26†	——
	Massachusetts	-21.37	.39	——	.68	-.33
	Ohio	103.96	.13	.88†	-.50	——
	Texas	10.05	-.01	2.20†	.68	——
LE/C	California	139.71	-1.62†	——	.01	——
	Connecticut	-68.45	1.00†	——	.99	.08
	Indiana	-73.16	.70†	——	1.50†	——
	Massachusetts	-14.37	.49†	——	.12	-.23
	Ohio	60.78	.51†	.36	-1.70†	——
	Texas	-101.62	.02	2.30†	.08	——
TE/P	California	146.61	.86	——	-2.17	——
	Connecticut	505.84	3.10	——	5.83	-1.62
	Indiana	96.09	.07	——	.62	——
	Massachusetts	164.42	2.15†	——	-5.27	1.95†
	Ohio	156.38	-.10	-1.08	-2.02	——
	Texas	281.91	.07	5.50†	-1.55	——
LE/P	California	-125.75	3.11	——	.39	——
	Connecticut	204.84	3.02	——	3.59	-1.18
	Indiana	24.00	1.35	——	-.23	——
	Massachusetts	187.16	2.82†	——	-8.31†	1.57
	Ohio	182.69	3.12†	-.47	-11.24†	——
	Texas	35.33	.18	7.81†	-1.20	——

| - - - - - - - | VARIABLES | | | | | | |
NON-W	MIGR	SAL	DEN	ADA	SEC	CAP	AUX
—	—	.28	—	-.05	.60†	—	.31
—	—	.08	—	.01	.93†	—	-3.78
—	—	.76	—	.00	.04	—	2.42†
—	—	-1.18	-.01	.02	.40†	-.24	.73
.32	—	.33	-.34	—	-.14	-.02	-1.77
—	—	.07	—	-.02	.36	—	.05
—	—	.23	—	.00	.39	—	-2.42
—	—	.52	—	.01	.16	—	1.91†
—	—	.12	.04	-.07	.15	-.30	.08
.03	—	.29	-.29	—	-.03	-.01	-1.12
—	-.99	5.49	-.56	-.02	1.83†	.22	-3.17
—	—	-18.30	—	.46	1.53	—	104.04†
—	—	2.51	—	.14†	2.25†	—	2.01
—	—	1.16	—	.01	3.28†	—	12.26†
—	—	.78	.25	.00	1.66†	10.61†	21.94
-.27	—	.53	-.46	—	.39	-.01	-1.25
—	-5.73	2.03	-.12	.13	1.34	-.73	29.94
—	—	-12.13	—	.71	2.61	—	77.92†
—	—	1.23	—	.11	1.26	—	8.57
—	—	.43	—	.06	3.59†	—	10.06†
—	—	5.63	.52	.00	-.50	.92	6.83
-.57	—	1.18	.25	—	.21	-.02	-4.50

* See Table 2 for an explanation of abbreviations and a description of variables.
† Significant at .95 level of probability under assumptions of simple random sampling, homogeneous variances, and other conditions for the application of conventional confidence intervals.

ysis, the model as a whole does not have great explanatory power. In the over-all analysis the proportion of variance explained for per capita expenditures is rather low, and the higher multiple regression coefficients for per pupil expenditures are attributable to the unanticipated strong effect of auxiliary services. In the state-by-state analysis, the same basic sets of independent variables yield widely divergent multiple correlation coefficients.

Several reasons may be advanced for the failure of the estimating equation to achieve a fairly high and regular explanation of variation in spending among local school systems. One possibility is that the fundamental assumption is false and the agencies that determine local school expenditures are not motivated by rational economic objectives. Therefore, local agencies do not respond in similar fashion to similar preference patterns. An alternative possibility is that the basic assumption is correct but that the model, as constructed, is not an effective means of revealing the underlying uniformities. Unfortunately, it is difficult to improve the model to provide a more satisfactory treatment of state arrangements which differ not only among states but among school systems within the same state. Other difficulties in the model are also inherent—substantial intercorrelations among independent variables, problems in accurate estimation of variables for noncoterminous school districts, and the identification problem for variables that have more than one kind of effect.

Simple and Multivariate Relationships

The results of the analysis provide a detailed set of simple and partial correlation coefficients between four categories of expenditures for local schools and a variety of factors. There is partial confirmation of some long-held notions such as that expenditures are lower in dependent school systems, even when ability to pay and cost elements are taken into account. However, doubt is cast on other equally traditional views. For example, school systems that contain a larger proportion of non-whites in the population do not spend less when other factors are included. Comparison of correlation coefficients among states reveals similarities in the effects of variables such as the proportion of pupils in secondary grades and great differences in the effects of others, for example, median family income.

Per Capita and Per Pupil Expenditures

State personal income per capita and the proportion of pupils in the population have strong positive effects on total per capita expenditures and considerably less influence on per pupil outlays.

Auxiliary services are of great importance in per pupil expenditures but have little effect on per capita spending. Most other variables have similar effects on both per capita and per pupil expenditures.

Total and Local Expenditures

The dominant theme of the results is the effect of state and federal aid as portrayed by the differences in coefficients for total and local expenditures. These differences show that among local school systems total expenditures are not responsive to variations in local ability to pay but do vary with cost conditions. Local expenditures, however, reflect community income levels but not differences in costs. The detailed pattern of the way in which state aid differentially affects the various factors associated with school spending and the description of the manner in which equalization occurs are among the major findings of this study.

Suggestions for Further Research

This analysis leaves a number of results still to be explained. Differences among states are particularly puzzling. A fruitful approach to the solution of this and of other unexplained points undoubtedly lies in an analytic examination of state aid arrangements. A classification based on a study of the responses of local school officials to various aspects of state aid is needed, rather than a classification by statute or by measures of the relative importance of different types of grants. In such a classification it probably will be necessary to go beyond differences among states and to distinguish the various state aid arrangements that apply to different types of school systems within the same state. Small school districts should be included in such an analysis. One possible approach would be first to classify in detail types of state aid programs and then to place a sample of school systems into appropriate categories. Analysis would then proceed to determine whether relationships between spending and state and local community characteristics are more regular within categories than among categories. If so, the classifications have explanatory power. An alternative methodology is to search for sets of school systems with similar relationships between expenditures and state and local characteristics, and then to examine state aid arrangements for each of the sets to determine whether there are categories of aid arrangements to match the observed similarities in relationships.

Although problems of the definition of the dependent variable, the specification of an over-all model, and the measurement of characteristics in noncoterminous jurisdictions still remain partially unresolved, the crucial requisite for an empirical theory of public expenditures is a method for the treatment of intergovermental relationships, especially those that involve grants-in-aid to relatively autonomous government units.

Finally, there are unresolved problems in the specification of demand variables for public expenditures. The preferences of citizens for public education and for other public-sector outlays may be revealed indirectly by measures of income and educational attainment. The research here has attempted to test the extent to which such variables are accurate measures of demand. But decisions about public expenditures are made by administrative and elected officials, not by citizens. Public demands may be imperfectly understood and imperfectly translated by such officials. The political process of resource allocation may or may not reflect accurately, in specific instances, the aggregate of household demands for public services and the additional demands for social benefits that may accrue from specific outlays. At the same time, it is possible that public officials may act on the basis of a different appraisal of the effects of education upon productivity and upon the future earnings of pupils than that held by parents and other members of the community. Under these circumstances, educational outlays would not be closely linked to demand by local households.

Research on the determinants of public expenditures, directed to an examination of the linkage between preferences for public goods and political decision processes, would be helpful in furthering an understanding of the politics and economics of resource allocation.

VI. Summary and Conclusions

THIS MONOGRAPH is an economic analysis of factors that influence expenditures by local public school systems from the point of view of both normative and positive economic approaches to individual and organizational behavior. Normative aspects of educational spending constitute the subject matter of the chapter that deals with criteria for economically optimum levels of spending in the context of a consumer directed economy. The positive side was examined in the discussion of empirical studies of the factors associated with public school spending and in the description and analysis of expenditures in a nationwide sample of local school systems. The normative analysis produces guidelines for the evaluation of expenditures for public schools, while the positive analysis indicates the extent to which actual spending conforms to normative standards and suggests some of the implications of economic, demographic, and social changes for future outlays for local public schools.

ACTUAL AND OPTIMUM PUBLIC EXPENDITURES FOR EDUCATION

Optimum Expenditures

A most important factor in the determination of optimum levels of educational expenditures is the widespread social and economic benefit from education which makes public rather than private finance of education essential. In addition, proper decisions about educational expenditures require that the total of all benefits be taken into account, and as a consequence, a pattern of solely local public finance will fail to register the global nature of the consequences of education in an interdependent market economy with a geographically mobile population.

Another crucial aspect is that the function of education in promoting social mobility and providing for equality of economic opportunity requires that educational attainment be divorced, substantially, from the individual family's capacity to pay and from its social position. To achieve desired ends with regard to opportunity it is often necessary for public decisions to countervene rather than conform to the preferences of parents in the provision of education. At the same time, in a society in which individual preferences are believed to be of great importance in social and economic decisions, the desires of individuals must be reflected in the amount and character of the educational services provided. There is no contradiction here if individual preferences are manifested through democratic political processes which lead to a solution based on consensus rather than through economic processes where the solution is based on an equilibrium for each participant or every family unit.

The nature of education as an economic good makes it difficult to fulfill the requisites of a social or even of an economic optimum. The indivisible character of the benefits of education, the impossibility of the exclusion of nonstudents from sizable gains from educational expenditures, and the desire to use education to break the cycle of poverty and lack of motivation among certain low-income groups would rule out the achievement of an optimum through the market principle, even if education were to be sold at prices which were adjusted for divergences between social and private elements. Provision and finance of education, thus, falls under the budget principle. However, as has been discussed in Chapter III, the inability to ascertain individual preferences by political rather than market arrangements and problems of weighting preferences of different persons even if known, makes it impossible to achieve an economic optimum through the budget principle.

In the practice of public finance, taxation of individuals must be based on broad general principles and not on the basis of an exact determination of benefits received from such services as education. Expenditures have to be determined by political consensus and not by a summation of individual demands at given prices in terms of tax payments. Under these circumstances the crucial requisite for the approximation of the optimum in actual expenditures is a political process through which an accurate evaluation can be made of the claims for resources for education in comparison with the claims for other public services. Taxation can then be based on criteria which roughly estimate benefits received after allowance has been made for income redistribution in accordance with the community's view of distributional justice.

The Organization of Education and the Principles of Optimization

The administration of public elementary and secondary education by local governments is an arrangement intended to combine public finance with the greatest responsiveness to individual preferences. At the same time, state contributions to local school revenues serve to reflect the wide geographic scope of the benefits of education. When state aid regulations lead to equalization of expenditures in terms of costs or ability to pay in local school systems, the additional objective of equality of educational opportunity is furthered. Thus, in the context of the present organization of education in the United States, decisions about expenditures can reflect individual preferences, take account of geographic and individual spillover effects, and equalize educational opportunities.

All school systems, however, do not or cannot make use of arrangements conducive to the achievement of optimum levels of expenditures. Some states have statewide school systems or such narrowly defined standards for local schools that preferences within the community have little effect on the character of local education. In other states local sources of finance predominate, so that there is no provision for geographical spillover benefits. Finally, where state aid to local schools is miniscule, or where states grant aid on the basis of local performance rather than on needs or resources, no equalization occurs. Thus, while the general framework for educational organization in the United States permits the application of certain principles of optimization, these methods are not always utilized.

Even when advantage is taken of the opportunities for approaching an optimum within the arrangements for public education that prevail in the United States, there are no direct provisions to take account of interstate spillovers, inequality of incomes among states, and the need for joint consideration of education and the full range of public needs and resources. Federal policies in noneducational areas may, however, indirectly achieve some of these effects.

Federal participation in the finance of local schools is the obvious remedy to the national spillovers of benefits and the inequality of ability to pay for education among states. Only at the federal level can action be taken to provide funds and to distribute the cost of education so that states with lower incomes can provide educational services of a scope and quality similar to those of wealthier states. Complete equalization may not be desirable or even desired, but whatever the extent of interstate educational equalization, only the federal government can accomplish the task. With regard to spillover effects through migration or market transactions, again it is the federal government which is in a position to register demands from and costs to areas outside the state.

Apart from issues of the separation of church and state, the fundamental problem in federal financial participation in local school affairs is the retention of a role for the preferences of persons in local communities. It is naive to insist that federal funds can be provided without any federal control over their use. Yet the view that federal intrusion into local school affairs means surrender of local prerogatives ignores the extent of local autonomy now retained in such programs as public welfare, urban renewal, and public housing where a common complaint is the lack of federal supervision over its own programs. A well-educated population is now a national responsibility; in the highly interdependent society of the United States in this second half of the twentieth century, low rates of economic growth, an ill-informed and irrational electorate, and a lack of trained manpower to achieve broad social and political goals are no longer local but national problems. The rationale for federal participation in local school finances is clear, and it is time to begin to test a program for federal assistance to local elementary and secondary education that leaves adequate leeway for local discretion. The initial plan should be evaluated periodically and modifications adopted as needed, but surely the skills of those familiar with the practice of a federal form of government can rise to this challenge.

The role of the federal government is only one aspect of the problem of optimum levels of educational outlays in the context of alternative public and private expenditures. An evaluation of relevant alternatives is impossible under governmental arrangements that compartmentalize decisions about expenditures for various public programs. A solution to this aspect of the organization of education requires multifunction governmental units with sufficient geographic extent to encompass the major benefits and costs of the functions they administer. But, various public functions have differential spatial impacts, and, if all projects are to be compared, the role for local decision making is virtually eliminated. The problem of the size, functional duties, and taxing powers for various units of government is an issue in the forefront of the theory and practice of public policy in the United States. The concern among public finance economists and political scientists is that most units of local government are too small, and the proliferation of governments with responsibility for special functions such as education, water, and sewage disposal is not likely to promote rational solutions to pressing problems. The remedy most often proposed is increased state participation in these functions combined with consolidation whenever possible and the creation of interstate compacts for problems which transcend state boundaries.[1]

[1] For a more optimistic view of the capacity of local government to resolve these problems, see Vincent Ostrom, Charles M. Tiebout, and Robert Warren, "The Organization of Government in Metropolitan Areas," LV *American Political Science Review* (December 1961), 831-42.

To this must be added a role for the federal government if, as is true for education, the function has broad national implications.

Two major lines for improvement emerge from a consideration of each of the important shortcomings of the existing organization of education in the United States. One is the introduction of the federal government into local school finance. Here the task for administrators is the creation of arrangements that will permit federal grants for local education based on national requirements for an educated and skilled citizenry which do not at the same time excessively hamper local prerogatives. The second is the adoption in all states of education laws that take account of statewide geographic spillover effects and at the same time provide a considerable measure of equalization among school systems.

DETERMINANTS OF EXPENDITURES AND CONDITIONS FOR AN OPTIMUM

Local Preferences

A major purpose of local administration of education in the United States is to give an opportunity for the preferences of residents to influence expenditures for education. Direct measures of preferences for education are not readily available, but characteristics of the population such as years of education, per cent of children in nonpublic schools, per cent non-white, and per cent moved into district in last five years are factors that may be closely associated with preferences.

The results of various analyses show that none of these measures exerts a strong effect on the expenditures of individual school systems. Most of the studies reported in Chapter III do not include elements that reflect preferences, although one study found that in states with higher proportions of non-whites and of pupils attending private schools ratios of expenditures to incomes are lower.[2] Although preferences of residents of local communities may shape the general character of the educational system, and determine the allocation of expenditures within the school system, there is little evidence that under present arrangements total expenditure levels vary in accordance with certain obvious measures of local attitudes toward schooling when other relevant factors are taken into account.

Equalization

A major conclusion from the empirical study reported here is that systems for state aid achieve considerable equalization within

[2] See discussion of the McMahon study, *supra*, pp. 55-56.

states. It is probable that equalization is the opposite side of the coin from the failure to find local preferences important in the explanation of expenditures. Despite arguments to the contrary, it appears that state regulations which foster equalization cannot help but reduce the role of local preferences in the determination of expenditures. Differences in total expenditures within states result largely from variations in the proportions of pupils, in costs, and in the extent of auxiliary services. These factors, for the most part, constitute the basis for state aid grants to equalize local burdens. In the process, the effects of factors that reflect local preferences seem to be virtually obliterated.

Perhaps a more direct approach by means of questionnaire surveys on attitudes toward public education would uncover more of an association between preferences and expenditures. However, if state aid measures that promote equalization inhibit the effectuation of local preferences, more refined measurements will not succeed in demonstrating a relationship that does not exist. The effects of local preferences, under these circumstances, may be noted only by examining, as the dependent variable, the composition of the educational services provided.

One apparent exception to equalization within states is the persistently lower total expenditure of dependent school systems. As has been argued in the previous chapter, the effect of state aid provisions appears to be a major determinant of these lower levels of spending.

The emphasis on equalization within states fails to bridge the gap between states with widely divergent per capita personal incomes and educational needs and costs. If equalization is to mean provision of an adequate minimum level of real school services regardless of local ability, needs, or costs, many states require financial assistance from outside sources. Federal grants-in-aid are the only means for transfers of the size necessary. On the other hand, if equalization is to mean the provision of equal public services throughout the country for equal tax burdens, then a federal program of educational grants weighted in favor of low-income states runs counter to equalization. There are many facets to the conflict between spatial equity in the sense of equal public services for equal tax payments and equity in the distribution sense. However, at bottom, the resolution of this conflict requires a decision: is public finance to be viewed solely as a substitute mechanism for the market and is it to stimulate, as far as possible, its results, or is public finance a political mechanism responsive to both political and market forces? Equalization among states is acceptable under the latter concept. It violates the market approach, however, and because it is not economically neutral it leads to such adjustments as migration to areas where a given level of public services costs less in taxes. The choice between distributional equity and economic neutrality cannot be resolved on analytic grounds; it is a question of social values.

External Effects

A finding that state action raises total expenditures to a level above that which would prevail if local factors alone determined outlays is evidence that external benefits of local education receive consideration. There is, unfortunately, no way to determine the level of educational spending in the absence of state regulation, but variables that deal with state aid can provide some indication of the effect of state participation in local school finances. According to this study, a larger fraction of public school revenues collected by the state is associated with higher levels of total per capita expenditures and lower levels of local per pupil and per capita outlays. It has little effect on per pupil spending. The variables for equalization and general-purpose aid are intended to gauge the effects of different types of state aid, and so do not indicate whether, in general, state aid has a positive or negative influence on expenditures.

Studies reported in Chapter III show the positive effect of intergovernmental revenue in city and state expenditures and support the conclusion that state participation in local school finance does raise total expenditures. Further, the strong positive effect reported here of statewide personal income on expenditures, in contrast to the weak association of local incomes, may be interpreted as evidence that in the absence of state action total expenditures would be considerably lower. On the other hand, it is also possible to conclude that in the absence of state action the positive effect of local incomes would be considerably greater.

The use of revenues from state sources for local education is strong evidence of a wide dispersal of the costs of local education. Still, it is necessary to compare the geographical and personal incidence of state and local taxation before concluding that geographical and personal spillovers have been taken into account by the tax structure. It can be argued, however, that state taxes generally are not returned dollar for dollar to the areas from which they are collected and usually encompass a wider range of taxpayers than does the property tax. Thus, since state taxation provides a substantial portion of revenues for local schools, there is a tendency for the costs of education to be spread among all the residents of a state and not only among those living within the boundaries of the school system.

Although state grants-in-aid and state taxation take account of certain external effects, there is little doubt that without a mechanism for the reflection of national benefits there is a substantial understatement of the external benefits of education and a consequent failure to reach optimum levels of expenditures for local schools.

THE FUTURE: EVENTS AND POLICY

The use of empirical studies such as those described in this monograph to anticipate future levels of educational expenditures is subject to a number of difficulties. First of all, it is necessary to select key independent factors and to determine their relationship, over time, to current expenditures for local schools. The studies reveal a good deal about these key factors, but cross-section relationships often do not show the effects of temporal changes, and relationships found for one period or at one point cannot be expected to remain unchanged as time passes. Secondly, forecasting requires assumptions about future values of the independent variables, and frequently these values cannot be predicted with accuracy.

In the discussion of future trends it is useful to distinguish those independent variables whose values can be influenced by public policy and those determined by forces outside the realm of choice. This distinction, of course, is not entirely determined by the nature of the variable, but also depends on the problem under study. For example, the age distribution of the population and per capita personal income are not policy or instrument variables for the study of local school spending, but there are situations in which these factors can be treated as capable of manipulation by policy measures. In the following brief discussion of the major factors likely to influence future current educational outlays in the United States, only intergovernmental grants, school system organization, and standards of school services are treated as instrument variables.

AUTONOMOUS OR NONPOLICY VARIABLES

Demographic Factors

The factor with the most clear-cut influence on future total spending for public education is the number of children enrolled in public schools. Public school enrollment is likely to grow at a rate slightly in excess of the rate of growth of the number of school-age children because both the proportion in nonpublic schools and the relative frequency of early school drop-outs show signs of falling. Per capita expenditures will rise if the proportion of school-age children increases, and evidence here indicates that per pupil expenditures will not be reduced. Further positive effects on both per capita and per pupil expenditures can be expected as the proportion of pupils in secondary grades grows. While there is no reason to expect an appreciable rise in the proportion of persons in the 14–18-year-old age group, it is probable that pressures for the completion of high school will increase considerably the proportion of pupils in secondary grades in certain less industrialized states.

Other demographic factors have been found important by some investigators. There is research to suggest that an increase in the proportion of non-whites in the population is accompanied by lower public outlays for education. However, the finding here is that when cost and demand factors are taken into account, it seems unlikely that the modest increase in the proportion of non-whites in the population that may occur in the future will lead to lower per capita or per pupil expenditures. On the contrary, it is quite possible that political factors may lead to a change in relationships so that areas which contain relatively large numbers of Negroes will receive increased grants-in-aid. This will bring larger expenditures for education, as part of a program to combat the high rates of delinquency and unemployment and the low wage levels now characteristic of many such areas.

Over-all density is bound to increase as population grows, but there is little evidence that spending for local public education will change as a consequence. The present study does not give any support to the view that increased density directly influences school outlays.

Two further demographic factors, years of education of adults and the proportion of families who have moved recently, were not found, in this study, to have a systematic influence on per capita or per pupil outlays in local school systems.

Income and Property

Apart from population characteristics, specific autonomous economic factors will shape future outlays for public education. The crucial elements here are the levels and distribution of income, and property valuations. Income and property values can be expected to increase during the next decade, but their rates of growth depend on a series of factors outside the control of local school governments.[3] Target rates of growth of GNP of 4½ to 5 per cent appear out of reach, and a rate of growth of 3 to 3½ per cent may not even be attained in the next decade.

As is generally true of research findings in other areas of public and private spending, estimates of the effect of income on expenditures for public schools are lower for cross-section studies than for time-series analyses. Previous time-series studies estimate the income elasticity of educational spending at about one for the period from 1900 to 1958, with a somewhat higher figure for the postwar years. Other cross-section studies, and the research here, find the income elasticity of different aspects of educational expenditures generally below one. The results of time-series studies are more directly applicable to projections of future expenditures, but they suffer from a failure to take explicit account of changes in key factors such as state aid arrangements during the period under study. Certain of these changes were intended to increase the responsiveness of educational expenditures to income. To anticipate similar increases in expenditures from subsequent rises in income may lead to overestimates.

Unless there are continued changes in arrangements for grants-in-aid and given present-day pressures for improved services for a wide range of local and state government functions, it is unlikely that the responsiveness of educational expenditures to changes in income will exceed an elasticity of one. If, however, a considerable reduction in federal taxation is enacted as an antirecession or growth stimulation measure, state and local governments may find it possible to capture some of these funds for local school finance. Such a situation would produce a higher response of educational expenditures to future increases in income.

Much of what has been said for income also holds for property valuation. Previous research studies generally show close relationships among assessed valuations, family income, and educational spending. The analysis of those states with equalized property values included in this study shows that, with an occasional exception, this variable has the highest partial correlation with all four categories of expenditures.

---

[3] A portion of future increases in national income and in the family incomes of residents of local communities can be attributed to present-day educational outlays, but it is certainly not possible to argue that local school officials can determine future levels of educational spending by current educational policies aimed at raising income and wealth in the future.

The postwar growth in educational expenditures was heavily financed out of the property tax, but there is continued discontent with this form of taxation and resistance in many communities to further increases in property tax rates. Increases in per capita or per pupil expenditures attributable to property valuation probably will come from increases in new construction rather than from increased tax rates or assessments on existing property. Revenue from existing property may increase, but only enough to maintain current levels of per pupil outlays in the face of larger enrollments.

POLICY PARAMETERS

Of the major factors which influence expenditures for local public schools, state aid arrangements, size and autonomy of local school governments, and perhaps the scope and quality of school services are subject to the discretion of public officials.

Scope and Quality of Education

To the extent that the scope and quality of educational services are determined by demand and cost factors they are not subject to manipulation by local officials and are thus not a policy parameter. The initial view in this study was that these elements were determined by expenditures and not vice versa. However, the extremely high partial correlations found for the number of auxiliary personnel per pupil indicate that this aspect of scope and quality has an effect separate from conventional demand or cost factors. There is evidence, therefore, that scope and quality are to some extent expenditure-determining rather than expenditure-determined, and thus constitute a policy variable.

An historical index of the number of principals, superintendents, and consultants per 1,000 pupils shows a steady rise throughout the twentieth century.[4] No doubt other measures of scope and quality would reveal similar increases. The pressures for stronger public school curricula probably will mount further in response to the current emphasis on the importance of human resources for the achievement of national economic and political goals. It is likely that the states will raise standards of instruction and curricula either by legal imposition on local school systems or by persuasion through the offers of matching grants, in accordance with techniques such as

[4] Werner Z. Hirsch, *Analysis of the Rising Costs of Public Education* (Washington: Joint Economic Committee, 1959), 29.

those now used by the federal government under the National Defense Education Act.

Organization of School Districts

Consolidation of local school districts long has been proposed as a cost-reducing measure. However, the continued failure to find substantiation for the presence of economies of scale in education makes it doubtful that future expenditures will be reduced by consolidation. Further, since 1942 the number of operating school systems has been reduced from over 100,000 to about 35,000, and there are strong barriers to the consolidation of the remaining small districts. Enlargement of the size of school systems may reduce costs but at the same time be accompanied by an expansion and improvement of educational services. The failure to find a negative association between enrollment and expenditures per pupil is not an argument against consolidation; it is, however, an indication that future trends in consolidation are unlikely to lead to a reduction in current outlays per pupil.

Greater autonomy for local school systems in taxation and expenditures has been a rallying cry for educational administrators who wish to raise outlays. Simple tabulations have shown that expenditures per pupil tend to be higher in independent school systems and the findings here assign a negative coefficient to dependent status in a multivariate analysis. Historically the porportion of pupils in independent school systems has been rising slightly as a consequence of the movement to the suburbs of families with school-age children. At the same time, in a few states the taxing powers of local school districts have been somewhat broadened. It is doubtful that a policy-determined shift in the status of present dependent systems would, in and of itself, raise expenditures. The dependent systems are mostly in large cities which face high levels of needs and costs for the entire range of locally provided public services. A shift in status would not eliminate these conditions, but might change state aid distributions so that school systems located in metropolitan areas would receive more aid, and other systems less.

Property Tax Reforms

There are two policy measures that center on taxation. These could provide a substantial once-and-for-all increase in revenues for local school systems and could, therefore, also increase their outlays. One is the reform of tax assessment procedures so that property valuations for tax purposes are more closely related to market values.

For a substantial effect such reform must be accompanied by higher over-all effective property tax rates, but removal of the considerable injustices that now characterize assessment procedures in most states might improve the climate for tax rate increases.

A second important reform would be to redefine school district boundaries so that no industrial enclaves and other business and commercial properties are sheltered from property taxation for local schools by specially drawn boundaries. The present tendency for tax concessions and special school district boundaries as an inducement to location of industry serves not only to widen the extent of such practices but also to prevent reform. At present there appear to be strong political resistances to reform of this sort; instead, state corporate income and other business taxes are used to obtain revenue from locally protected industries. Statewide taxes apply equally to all firms, but those sheltered from the local property tax continue to avoid paying their full share of local tax burdens.

Grants-in-Aid

Intergovernmental transfers are generally thought of as the instrument with the greatest potential for influencing educational policies. The analysis here does not include the amount of state aid as an independent variable, but does find that a higher proportion of revenue from state and federal sources has a positive influence on total per capita outlays and a strong negative effect on local expenditures.

To a considerable extent state aid is a substitute for local educational expenditures, and the receipt of state aid for local schools permits the use of local tax revenues for other public functions, such as police and fire protection, which are generally less strongly supported by state grants-in-aid. Thus, to raise per capita or per pupil educational outlays through state aid may require an increase in grants by as much as five dollars per pupil to raise total spending per pupil by one dollar. The consequences of efforts to raise per pupil spending through such an expansion of state aid might be desirable because of the improvement in other public services which would be the beneficiaries of reduced pressures on local revenues for funds for education.

This indirect approach, however, is not an efficient solution to the general problem of local government finance. Intergovernmental grants should be based on costs, needs, and ability to pay for all local government functions, not only for education. State aid as a policy parameter for education should be viewed in the broad context of the finance of all local government functions and not as a matter of trying to get as much as possible for education without regard for other public functions. Acceptance of this principle implies recognition of the need for extensive revision of existing state aid statutes throughout the nation with a view to the integration of grants-in-aid for education with grants for other local public services.

Consideration of the amount of state aid as a policy or instrument variable is not without objection. As has been argued in Chapter III, under a given set of state aid arrangements, historical changes in levels of state grants-in-aid are very closely tied to changes in state per capita personal income. Thus, unless state aid statutes are substantially revised, changes in levels of income are likely to determine, within fairly narrow limits, future levels of intergovernmental grants. Intergovernmental revenues as a proportion of total revenues for local schools are, on the other hand, more a matter of policy, but apparently this fraction does not influence total per pupil outlays.

There is a paradox that emerges from this investigation of policy variables to influence expenditures for local public schools. Those variables whose effects are known, such as population growth, percentage of pupils in high school, state per capita personal income, and even level of state aid per pupil, are not subject to manipulation through policy decisions. The major instrumental variable, alternative state aid arrangements, however, is the factor about whose effects least is known.

APPENDIX TABLE 1
Matrix of Correlations Among Independent Variables[*][‡]

VARIABLE	Y	Y+	Y/C†	PROP C†	CHILD	PRIV	ED	NON-W	MIGR	SAL
Y	1.00	.70	.52	.42	-.20	.42	.44	-.46	.19	.55
Y+		1.00	.55	.40	-.20	.45	.51	-.40	.22	.55
Y/C†			1.00	.73	-.37	.43	.39	-.62	.14	.78
PROP/C†				1.00	-.22	.26	.35	-.51	.31	.69
CHILD					1.00	-.28	-.22	.37	.07	-.27
PRIV						1.00	.29	-.39	-.06	.48
ED							1.00	-.37	.25	.42
NON-W								1.00	-.18	-.52
MIGR									1.00	.22
SAL										1.00
SMSA										
DEN										
ADA										
CAP										
SEC										
AUX										
DEP										
SR/TR†										
EA/TA†										
GPA/TA†										

SMSA	DEN	ADA	CAP	SEC	AUX	DEP	SR TR†	EA TA†	GPA TA†	UNWEIGHTED MEAN
.42	.24	.03	.01	.06	.23	-.02	-.48	-.04	.03	55.57
.49	.29	.04	-.01	.05	.26	-.05	-.48	-.06	.04	14.71
.39	.24	.03	.04	.02	.36	.11	-.74	-.15	.09	21.71
.24	.13	.01	-.02	-.05	.20	-.16	-.59	-.24	.24	41.83
-.11	-.32	-.10	-.05	-.12	-.17	-.20	.64	-.04	-.05	37.27
.38	.39	.11	.04	.11	.22	.08	-.56	.00	.01	12.33
.34	.13	.01	-.03	.02	.15	-.05	-.39	.00	-.02	10.46
-.27	-.10	.06	-.05	-.02	-.25	-.13	.64	-.04	-.05	11.77
.12	-.07	-.05	-.04	-.10	-.01	-.19	-.04	-.10	.09	17.21
.41	.28	.06	-.01	.04	.32	-.10	-.68	-.06	.08	40.17
1.00	.39	.16	.02	.01	.16	.00	-.32	.02	.00	.41
	1.00	.36	.00	.09	.16	.03	-.22	.02	.03	16.04
		1.00	-.02	.02	-.03	.03	.00	.04	.03	80.78
			1.00	.00	.09	.08	-.05	.02	-.05	60.89
				1.00	.19	.02	-.01	.14	-.04	32.18
					1.00	.08	-.27	-.01	-.05	1.67
						1.00	-.12	-.29	-.06	.28
							1.00	.07	.10	45.36
								1.00	.11	56.68
									1.00	77.78

* See Table 2 for an explanation of abbreviations and a description of variables.
† Variable differs from state to state, but is constant for all school systems within a state.
‡ These correlations and means are for the 1127 school systems that were used in the analysis of total per pupil expenditures. Some of these school systems were not included in the other analyses because of missing data or because they are not organized on a K-12 basis. The values for the correlations and means found here, therefore, are similar to but not identical with those for the school systems included in the analyses of total and local per capita and local per pupil expenditures.

Index

Ability to pay, 75
Adaptability, 60-61, 67-68
Advisory Commission on Intergovernmental Relations, 75n
Aggregate demand, 18-20
Alabama, 2
Alaska, 2
Amortization, 70
Arkansas, 2
Auxiliary services, 84, 100-01, 104, 119, 125
Average cost, 14

Benefits of education, 3, 27-28
Benefit principle, 11-13, 140
Benson, Charles S., 26n, 33n
Berolzheimer, Joseph, 40n, 43, 44, 55, 70n
Beta coefficient, 93-94, 95
Bloomberg, Warner, Jr., 86n
Bowen, Howard R., 10n, 14n
Brazer, Harvey E., 45-48, 64-65, 67, 70n, 75
Budget principle, 12-13
Burkhead, Jesse, 5n

California, 2, 46, 47, 48, 51, 59, 130, 131
Capital expenditures, 69-70
Carroll, John J., 75n
Census data, 90-91
Church-state, 141
City expenditures, 64-65
Cleveland, 46, 53, 63-64
Colm, Gerhard, 41n, 43, 44, 55, 55n
Commission on Intergovernmental Relations, 21n
Competition, in market economy, 9-11
Connecticut, 130, 131
Consolidation of districts, 150
Consumer demand, 12-13; for education, 27-28; for public goods, 21; for schools, 25-26
Consumer sovereignty, 17, 26
Cornell, Francis G., 60

Cost: of education, 27-28; differences among regions, 77, 77n; variables, 97
Cross section analysis, 39, 68-69, 74

Dahl, R. A., 13n
Davenport, Donald, 41n
Debt service, 70, 75, 96n, 119, 130
Decision-making process, local, 86-87; see also political process
Decreasing cost, 14-15
Delaware, 93n
Demand for education, 29
Demographic factors, 146-47
Denison, Edward F., 29n
Density, as a determinant, 44, 55-56, 147
Dependent and independent variables, 37-39; dependent variables in the model, 69-73
Dewhurst, J. Frederic, 40, 40n
Downs, Anthony, 66

Eckstein, Otto, 41n, 54n
Economic growth, 17-21; and education, 29
Economic model, 131-36
Economic stability, 17-21
Economies of scale, 47-48, 62-63, 83, 125, 131
Education, as an economic good, 3-4, 140; as consumption, 35-36; as investment, 35-36; effects on production, 28-29
Efficiency, economic, 8-9, 13, 16; in educational production, 82-83; in market economy, 8; in schools, 24; technological, 8-9
Elasticity of expenditures for education, see income elasticity of demand for education
Equalization, 143-44
Expenditures: among cities, 45-48; among local governments, 45-48; among school systems, 60-65; among states, 43-45; education, growth in, 49-54; government, growth

157